TEEN RIGHTS AND FREEDOMS

I Electronic Devices

TEEN RIGHTS AND FREEDOMS

I Electronic Devices

Sylvia Engdahl
Editor

GREENHAVEN PRESS
A part of Gale, Cengage Learning

GALE
CENGAGE Learning·

Detroit • New York • San Francisco • New Haven, Conn • Waterville, Maine • London

Elizabeth Des Chenes, *Director, Publishing Solutions*

© 2012 Greenhaven Press, a part of Gale, Cengage Learning

For more information, contact:
Greenhaven Press
27500 Drake Rd.
Farmington Hills, MI 48331-3535
Or you can visit our Internet site at gale.cengage.com.

For product information and technology assistance, contact us at:

Gale Customer Support, 1-800-877-4253.
For permission to use material from this text or product, submit all requests online at www.cengage.com/permissions.

Further permissions questions can be emailed to permissionrequest@cengage.com.

Articles in Greenhaven Press anthologies are often edited for length to meet page requirements. In addition, original titles of these works are changed to clearly present the main thesis and to explicitly indicate the author's opinion. Every effort is made to ensure the Greenhaven Press accurately reflects the original intent of the authors. Every effort has been made to trace the owners of copyrighted material.

Cover Image © Darko Zelijkovic/Shutterstock.com.

LIBRARY OF CONGRESS CATALOGING-IN-PUBLICATION DATA

Electronic devices / Sylvia Engdahl, book editor.
    p. cm. -- (Teen rights and freedoms)
    Includes bibliographical references and index.
    ISBN 978-0-7377-5825-2 (hbk.)
  1. Video games and teenagers. 2. Cell phones and teenagers. 3. Internet and teenagers. 4. Electronics--Social aspects. I. Engdahl, Sylvia.
    HQ784.V53E44 2012
    303.48'33--dc23

                                           2012006788

Printed in the United States of America
1 2 3 4 5 6 7 16 15 14 13 12

Contents

to children and teens, ruling that it violated the First Amendment rights of those whose parents did not object to such games. Games are a form of free speech, said the Court, and they contain no more violence than many books given to children.

dents at schools where they are banned nevertheless bring their phones with them every day.

Alex Howard

A teen who is not permitted to use cell phones in class says that he and other students do it anyway. He believes teachers actually cause more disruption when they interrupt class to punish cell phone users. In his opinion, phone calls in class should be prohibited, but not texting, and his school's outdated policy should be questioned.

Colleen Gillard

Although most schools have forbidden the use of cell phones in class, some allow students to text answers to quizzes and other written assignments. This enables them—and their teachers—to receive instant feedback. Moreover, since most students already have phones, it is especially useful where schools and families cannot afford to buy computers.

Michael Pines

An attorney warns that when serious harm results from texting while driving, the violator can be put in jail. He describes ten of the worst accidents that have occurred, many of which involved teens either as drivers or as victims, and tells what happened to the drivers. One eighteen-year-old girl who killed an elderly woman was sentenced to up to ten years in prison.

they drive and where they go, in addition to using software to monitor their Internet activity. Privacy laws do not protect teens from parental spying, and many parents believe such devices are justified for safety reasons.

there have been thousands of illegal downloads of her second book and because her sales dropped, her publisher may not accept any more books by her in the future.

Foreword

*"In the truest sense freedom cannot be
bestowed, it must be achieved."*
                    Franklin D. Roosevelt,
                    September 16, 1936

The notion of children and teens having rights is a relatively recent development. Early in American history, the head of the household—nearly always the father—exercised complete control over the children in the family. Children were legally considered to be the property of their parents. Over time, this view changed, as society began to acknowledge that children have rights independent of their parents, and that the law should protect young people from exploitation. By the early twentieth century, more and more social reformers focused on the welfare of children, and over the ensuing decades advocates worked to protect them from harm in the workplace, to secure public education for all, and to guarantee fair treatment for youths in the criminal justice system. Throughout the twentieth century, rights for children and teens—and restrictions on those rights—were established by Congress and reinforced by the courts. Today's courts are still defining and clarifying the rights and freedoms of young people, sometimes expanding those rights and sometimes limiting them. Some teen rights are outside the scope of public law and remain in the realm of the family, while still others are determined by school policies.

Each volume in the Teen Rights and Freedoms series focuses on a different right or freedom and offers an anthology of key essays and articles on that right or freedom and the responsibilities that come with it. Material within each volume is drawn from a diverse selection of primary and secondary sources— journals, magazines, newspapers, nonfiction books, organization newsletters, position papers, speeches, and government documents, with a particular emphasis on Supreme Court and lower court decisions. Volumes also include first-person narratives from young people and others involved in teen rights issues, such as parents and educators. The material is selected and arranged to highlight all the major social and legal controversies relating to the right or freedom under discussion. Each selection is preceded by an introduction that provides context and background. In many cases, the essays point to the difference between adult and teen rights, and why this difference exists.

Many of the volumes cover rights guaranteed under the Bill of Rights and how these rights are interpreted and protected in regard to children and teens, including freedom of speech, freedom of the press, due process, and religious rights. The scope of the series also encompasses rights or freedoms, whether real or perceived, relating to the school environment, such as electronic devices, dress, Internet policies, and privacy. Some volumes focus on the home environment, including topics such as parental control and sexuality.

Numerous features are included in each volume of Teen Rights and Freedoms:

- An annotated **table of contents** provides a brief summary of each essay in the volume and highlights court decisions and personal narratives.
- An **introduction** specific to the volume topic gives context for the right or freedom and its impact on daily life.
- A brief **chronology** offers important dates associated with the right or freedom, including landmark court cases.
- **Primary sources**—including personal narratives and court decisions—are among the varied selections in the anthology.
- **Illustrations**—including photographs, charts, graphs, tables, statistics, and maps—are closely tied to the text and chosen to help readers understand key points or concepts.

- An annotated list of **organizations to contact** presents sources of additional information on the topic.
- A **for further reading** section offers a bibliography of books, periodical articles, and Internet sources for further research.
- A comprehensive subject **index** provides access to key people, places, events, and subjects cited in the text.

Each volume of Teen Rights and Freedoms delves deeply into the issues most relevant to the lives of teens: their own rights, freedoms, and responsibilities. With the help of this series, students and other readers can explore from many angles the evolution and current expression of rights both historic and contemporary.

Introduction

It is hardly news to teens that the use of electronic devices has become a fundamental part of living. To many—but by no means all—adults, however, it seems strange and upsetting that these devices are often favored over face-to-face contact. They worry because absorption with electronic connections seems to be replacing interest in "real life." Yet to the majority of teens and a growing number of their elders, immersion in the world of the Internet and cell phone communication *is* real life, no less real than the activities their grandparents enjoyed.

Contrary to what many people assume, this controversy is not a conflict between youth and age. Rather, it is part of a major transformation of human thought, perhaps no lesser than the transformation brought about by the invention of the printing press in the fifteenth century. Many scholars and philosophers have written about this subject. Some believe that the switch to electronic media is not a change for the better, and important abilities of the human mind are being lost. Others believe this change is a step forward, leading to the development of significant new capabilities.

Today's teens are living at a time when this change is progressing rapidly. The World Wide Web was not invented until 1990 and was not used by the general public until the advent of the first graphical browser in 1993. Cell phones were owned only by the wealthy until the 1990s, and teens rarely had them before the turn of the twenty-first century; the percentage of teen cell phone owners nearly doubled between 2004 and 2008.

Technological change is upsetting to a society, and since it inevitably involves loss as well as gain, it is always deplored by some people, even when welcomed by the majority. Before the ability to read and write became common, history was preserved by an oral tradition involving memorization of long narratives, often in the form of poetry. Not everyone liked the thought of the abandonment of this tradition. In the ancient Greek philosopher Plato's dialogue *Phaedrus*, one of the characters says regretfully of writing: "It will implant forgetfulness in [men's] souls: they will cease to exercise memory because they rely on that which is written, calling things to remembrance no longer from within themselves, but by means of external marks." Whether Plato personally believed this has long been debated, for he was a writer and in another book he said that poets—that is, bards who relied on memorized narrative—would be banned from his ideal republic. But it certainly represents a view held by some of his contemporaries.

The advent of printing also met opposition, for the authorities of the time realized that the wide availability of books would undermine the established political and religious order—as indeed it did. Later, television, which spread to homes during the 1940s and 1950s, was greeted with enthusiasm by the general public but viewed skeptically by traditionalists who believed TV would be numbing to the mind. All these developments changed the way people lived, just as the Internet and cell phone revolution have more recently. Not surprisingly, people who remember the way things used to be have mixed feelings about such changes, even when they themselves adopt the new technologies.

Although most adults today use electronic media, many are uncomfortable when they observe that young people know no other way to live. They feel that there is something missing from their children's lives. Perhaps there is; that is an issue about which experts disagree.

Do teens have any rights as to what electronic devices they use and how much time they spend using them? Legally, no. Minors are legally required to follow any rules, short of child abuse, that their parents or guardians impose—and, within limitations set by the Constitution, those imposed by schools. Teens often speak of a right to privacy, but this is a moral right, the extent of which depends on family agreements, rather than a legal one.

Neither are there any specific legal limitations on teen use of electronic devices except, in some states, a ban on cell phone use while driving, and in a few, recent laws against cyberbullying. Federal legislation in both these areas is under consideration. A proposed federal cyberbullying law would make it illegal to use electronic devices to "coerce, intimidate, harass or cause other substantial emotional distress."

However, all citizens, including teens, are obliged to obey general laws. Those who cause serious accidents by texting while driving can be charged with reckless endangerment or even sent to prison for vehicular homicide. Furthermore, many teens are unaware that sharing nude or sexually explicit pictures electronically is a violation of child pornography laws under which they can be convicted as sex offenders.

Another law commonly violated is the copyright law. Most teens know that it is illegal to download copyrighted music or e-books without permission, but they do it anyway. When caught, they can be sued for large sums of money, even years after the offense occurs. When not caught, the issue of conscience remains. Whether it is unethical to download without paying is a controversial question; some commentators—and even some artists—believe it is not, but the vast majority consider it a form of cheating that hurts not only the artists whose work is stolen but the music industry as a whole if sales of recordings continue to decline.

Similar to illegal downloading, the issue of conscience also arises when teens use electronic media to cheat in school. Many teens believe that using electronic devices to cheat is less dishonest than other forms of cheating. Polls show that many high school and college students use cell phones to cheat on exams, and most of them do not to consider it cheating in the same sense as copying from something handwritten.

There have always been people who cheat and people who disobey rules; today's technology simply makes it easier to do so, just as it makes constructive activity easier. Electronic devices are no more than tools. Perhaps in the future they will possess artificial intelligence capable of independent action, but until such time, all decisions about their use will be made by human beings who bear responsibility for those decisions. This is as true of moral responsibility as of responsibility for the role of such devices in daily living.

Nicholas Carr, a critic of the electronic culture, writes in his book *The Shallows: What the Internet Is Doing to Our Brains*, "People seem to be looking for ways to loosen technology's grip on their lives and thoughts. . . . I was particularly struck by the large number of notes that came from young people— high-schoolers, college kids, twentysomethings. They fear that constant connectivity may be constricting rather than expanding their horizons."

But, say supporters of the new culture, no one is forced to connect against his or her will. Human beings are free to choose what they will and will not do with the technologies available to them.

Chronology

1983	The first commercial cell phone system begins operating in Chicago and the Baltimore/Washington, DC corridor.
1985	There are about 340,000 cell phone subscribers in the United States.
1990	The cost of cell phone service decreases and subscribers surpass 5 million.
1992	The first experimental text message is sent to a cell phone.
1993	The first smartphone is released to the public.
1995	GPS tracking becomes available for civilian use.
	Cell phone users to whom texting is available average less than half a text message per month.
1998	The first mass-produced portable digital audio player is introduced.
1998	The first portable e-book readers are introduced. They are followed by the Sony Reader in 2006, the Kindle in 2007, the Nook in 2009, and the iPad in 2010.

2000   Wireless subscribers exceed 100 million, totaling approximately 38 percent of the US population.

2001   In *A&M Records v. Napster*, the US Court of Appeals for the Ninth Circuit rules that peer-to-peer music sites are guilty of copyright infringement if they fail to prevent the illegal sharing of MP3 files, thus causing the popular site Napster to shut down. Similar sites soon try to get around this ruling by not storing any files on their own servers.

The first iPod is released.

2002   Camera phones are first introduced in the US market.

Students are first caught using texting to cheat on a school exam (at Hitotsubashi University in Japan).

2003   The Recording Industry Association of America (RIAA) begins suing individuals it believes have illegally downloaded music, including a twelve-year-old girl whose case attracts widespread media attention.

2004   Forty-five percent of American adolescents ages twelve to seventeen have a cell phone, compared to 65 percent of adults.

2005

In *MGM v. Grokster*, the US Supreme Court rules that file-sharing networks that encourage illegal downloading can be sued for copyright infringement even if they do not store the files on their own servers and if their software also has legal uses.

Cell phone subscribers reach nearly 208 million, which is approximately 69 percent of the total US population. Subscribers use more than 1.5 trillion voice minutes and send and receive more than 81 billion text messages.

2007

Apple launches the iPhone.

Washington becomes the first of many states to pass a law banning texting while driving.

In *U.S. v. Finley,* the US Court of Appeals for the Fifth Circuit rules that police do not need a warrant to search the internal phone records and text messages on a cell phone seized from a person during a lawful arrest. (This decision does not apply to all states.)

2008

Seventy-one percent of American adolescents ages twelve to seventeen have a cell phone; 77 percent have a game console such as an Xbox or a PlayStation; 74 percent own an iPod or MP3 player; 55 percent have a portable gaming device.

2009   The Supreme Court of Ohio rules that police must have a warrant to search a cell phone. (The law differs from state to state.)

At least four states pass laws concerning sexting between minors, establishing lesser penalties than those imposed on adults for possession of child pornography. Many other states follow suit.

2010   In *Maverick Recording Company v. Harper*, the US Court of Appeals for the DC Circuit rules that college student Whitney Harper must pay $27,750 for copyright infringement of thirty-seven songs that she shared illegally on a peer-to-peer network when she was between the ages of fourteen and sixteen.

In the consolidated case *U.S. v. Maynard*, the US Court of Appeals for the DC Circuit rules that police may not place a GPS tracking device on a car without a warrant, and the government appeals. (The US Supreme Court agreed to decide the issue in *U.S. v. Jones* in 2012.)

Half of all US teens send fifty or more text messages a day; 15 percent of teen texters send more than two hundred per day.

2011   In *Brown v. Entertainment Merchants Association*, the US Supreme Court rules that laws prohibiting the sale of violent video games to minors are unconstitutional.

> *"With more than 1 billion text messages sent each day, it is no surprise that 42% of teens say they can text blindfolded."*

Most Teens Believe Wireless Devices Improve Their Lives

Harris Interactive

The following report on a Harris Interactive poll reveals that 57 percent of teens believe mobile devices improve life and nearly half consider their cell phones essential to their social lives. Four out of five carried a wireless phone in 2008 and felt that it gave them a sense of security. Teens favor texting over talking because of the speed and option to multitask. The teens surveyed expressed the hope that mobile devices of the future will allow even greater access. They also want phones with endless power, better security, and privacy.

Nearly half (47%) of US teens say their social life would end or be worsened without their cell phone, and nearly six in 10 (57%) credit their mobile device with improving their life, according to a national survey from CTIA [Cellular Telecommunications and Internet Association] and Harris Interactive.

Four out of five teens (17 million) carry a wireless device (a 40% increase since 2004), finds the study titled "Teenagers: A

Cell phones are key to young people's social lives. © AP Images/Jim Hannon.

Generation Unplugged," which probes how the growing teen wireless segment is using wireless products and how they want to use them in the future.

- A majority (57%) of teens view their cell phone as the key to their social life.

- Second only to clothing, teens say, a person's cell phone tells the most about their social status or popularity, outranking jewelry, watches and shoes.

Providing Entertainment and Security

- More than half of the respondents (52%) agree that the cell phone has become a new form of entertainment.

- One-third of teens play games on their phone.

- 80% say their cell phone provides a sense of security while on the go, confirming that the cell phone has become their mobile safety net when needing a ride (79%), getting important information (51%), or just helping out someone in trouble (35%).

- Teens carry cell phones to have access to friends, family and current events.

- Though only one in five (18%) teens care to pinpoint the location of their family and friends via their cell phone, 36% hate the idea of a cell phone feature that allows others to know their exact location.

Texting Replacing Talking

The study also confirmed that texting is replacing talking among teens. Teens admitted spending nearly an equal amount of time talking as they do texting each month. The feature is so important to them that if texting were no longer an option 47% of teens say their social life would end or be worsened—that's especially so among females (54% vs. 40%).

Teens say texting has advantages over talking because it offers more options, including multitasking, speed, the option to avoid verbal communication, and because it is fun—in that order, according to the study.

With more than 1 billion text messages sent each day, it is no surprise that 42% of teens say they can text blindfolded, the study found.

"Teens have created a new form of communication. We call it texting, but in essence it is a reflection of how teens want to communicate to match their lifestyles. It is all about multitasking, speed, privacy and control," said Joseph Porus, VP & chief architect [of the] Technology Group [at] Harris Interactive. "Teens in this study are crying for personalization and control of exactly what a wireless device or plan can do for them."

Devices of the Future

The survey asked teens what future changes they'd like to see in wireless services and devices and found that respondents want cell phones that break boundaries and are personalized to fit their lifestyles.

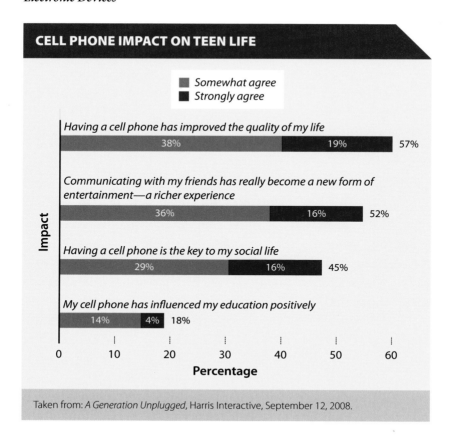

CELL PHONE IMPACT ON TEEN LIFE

■ Somewhat agree
■ Strongly agree

Having a cell phone has improved the quality of my life
38% | 19% | 57%

Communicating with my friends has really become a new form of entertainment—a richer experience
36% | 16% | 52%

Having a cell phone is the key to my social life
29% | 16% | 45%

My cell phone has influenced my education positively
14% | 4% | 18%

Impact

0   10   20   30   40   50   60
Percentage

Taken from: *A Generation Unplugged*, Harris Interactive, September 12, 2008.

Teens remain excited and openminded about the wireless possibilities and their ideal future mobile devices would feature five applications—phone, MP3 player, GPS, laptop computer and video player, according to Harris.

Also on teens' wish lists are phones that . . .

- Guarantee secured data access to the user only (80%)

- Provide accessibility to personal health records (66%)

- Present opportunities to be educated anywhere in the world (66%)

- Bring users closer to global issues impacting teens' world (63%)

- Are shockproof and waterproof (81%)
- Have endless power (80%)
- Feature a privacy screen (58%)
- Are made of flexible material and fold into different shapes and sizes (39%)
- Have artificial intelligence—ask it questions and it gives answers (38%)

"In the future, mobility for teens means mobile banking, mobile voting, location based services, personal entertainment—the sky is the limit for how mobile our lifestyles can be," said Steve Largent, president and CEO [of the] CTIA–The Wireless Association. "We've certainly come a long way in 25 years and expect teens to be a growth driver for the industry and have a major impact on the wireless landscape for years to come."

About the study: The study was conducted online in July 2008 among a nationally representative sample of 2,089 teenagers (age 13–19) across the US who have cell phones. More than 100 questions were asked on mobile phone usage, attitudes, behaviors, and teens' desires and aspirations for the future of mobile communications, entertainment, and other features.

> "What makes for addiction is when young people cannot extricate themselves from an activity in order to do the things required of them."

Teens Can Become Addicted to Electronic Devices

Stanton Peele

In the following viewpoint, Stanton Peele, a psychologist who has written many books about the problem of addiction, points out that young people can be addicted to many things besides drugs, including electronic devices. It is not the amount of time spent with them that indicates addiction, however, it is whether the activity produces emotional satisfaction that cannot be obtained any other way and interferes with other important aspects of life. In his opinion, addiction occurs in people who are unable to cope with their lives.

People become addicted to experiences that protect them from life challenges they can't deal with. It is not possible to say that any one thing causes addiction. Most kids who use drugs and alcohol don't become addicted to them. On the other hand, they can get addicted to very typical, common activities—such as eating, the Internet, other media, games, even medications they are prescribed for other problems.

The core of an addiction is that people become enmeshed in an activity that interferes with their functioning and, for children, thwarts their growth. If your children avoid regular involvements and experiences, if they can't cope with their lives, and if you fear that, left to their own devices, they will either collapse or go haywire, your children face addictive problems.

Disagreements about the nature of addiction make for vast differences in how we go about combating it. I do not find it helpful to regard addiction as a disease, which is the prevalent view these days. Although many people, including scientists, now believe that a wide range of things can be addictive, they wrongly persist in seeing addiction as a biological phenomenon beyond people's control.

By contrast, I was one of the first proponents of the view that addiction is not limited to drugs. But its very universality makes it clear that addiction can't be traced to a specific neurological mechanism. If sex or gambling addictions are defined by changes in the brain, why do so many people who find these involvements alluring for a moment, or even enthralling for some time, then simply move on to other activities? As we shall see, the exact same thing is true of "addictive" drugs.

Addiction can be especially debilitating for the young, but young people are more likely than not to outgrow it. The way out of addiction is to develop a range of skills and engage fully in life. The disease mythology is particularly unhelpful for young people. Telling adolescents that they have inherited addiction as part of their biological makeup encourages them to get stuck in the problem, rather than motivating them to overcome it.

Although my view of addiction is not the conventional one, my way of thinking has been adopted by many and is gaining influence in the field. My approach includes recognizing that addiction is not limited to drugs, that people overcome addiction when they are motivated and when their lives improve, and that successful therapy for addiction builds on people's own motivation to change while teaching them better ways of coping.

Defining Addiction

At the same time that not all drug use is addictive, addiction does not have to involve drugs. People can become addicted to powerful experiences such as sex, love, gambling, shopping, food—indeed, any experience that can absorb their feelings and consciousness. Addiction to the Internet is now in the spotlight, and before that came addiction to television and then video games.

Addictions provide quick, sure, easy-to-obtain gratifications, and advances in the electronic age such as the Internet, cell phone, iPod, and BlackBerry bring more addictive possibilities. Two addictions intertwined with the Internet are pornography and gambling. People become enmeshed in these experiences in isolation, rejecting everything else in their lives. A typical Internet pornography addiction case reads like this:

> My son is addicted to pornography. He can't stop looking at porn. He stays up on his computer all night. In the morning he can't stay awake, and he often doesn't go to school. I'm at my wits' end.

Likewise, we frequently hear of people who cannot stop gambling or shopping, often going deeply in debt. Such addicts, as adults, may steal, go to prison, and lose their families as a result. . . .

If we want to understand all kinds of self-destructive behaviors, we need a broader conception of addiction than the simple idea that some drugs are addictive: Addiction is a way of relating to the world. It is a response to an experience people get from some activity or object. They become absorbed in this experience because it provides them with essential emotional rewards, but it progressively limits and harms their lives. Six criteria define an addictive experience:

- It is powerful and absorbs people's feelings and thoughts.
- It can be predictably and reliably produced.
- It provides people with essential sensations and emotions

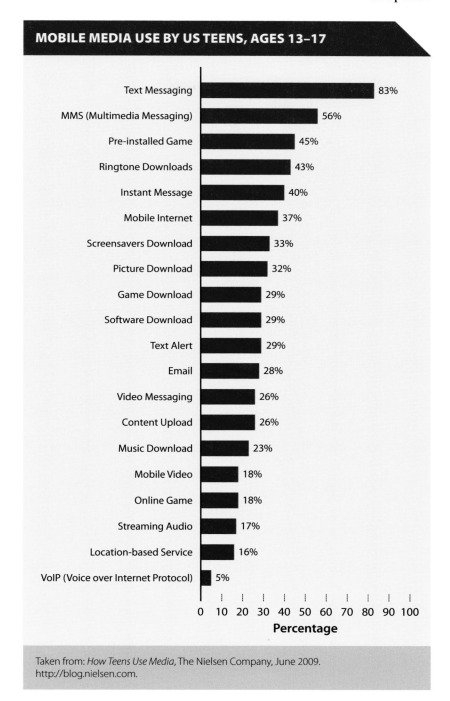

MOBILE MEDIA USE BY US TEENS, AGES 13–17

Category	Percentage
Text Messaging	83%
MMS (Multimedia Messaging)	56%
Pre-installed Game	45%
Ringtone Downloads	43%
Instant Message	40%
Mobile Internet	37%
Screensavers Download	33%
Picture Download	32%
Game Download	29%
Software Download	29%
Text Alert	29%
Email	28%
Video Messaging	26%
Content Upload	26%
Music Download	23%
Mobile Video	18%
Online Game	18%
Streaming Audio	17%
Location-based Service	16%
VoIP (Voice over Internet Protocol)	5%

Percentage

Taken from: *How Teens Use Media*, The Nielsen Company, June 2009.
http://blog.nielsen.com.

(such as feeling good about themselves, or the absence of worry or pain).

- It produces these feelings only temporarily, for the duration of the experience.
- It ultimately degrades other involvements and satisfactions.
- Finally, since they are getting less from their lives when away from the addiction, people are forced increasingly to return to the addictive experience as their only source of satisfaction.

Addiction vs. Normal Experience

Watching television every night, drinking daily (for an adult), and having an active social life are not necessarily addictions. Broadening the definition of addiction does not mean that everybody is addicted to something. The word is now often used casually, even humorously: a friend says he is addicted to crossword puzzles, a baby is addicted to his pacifier, a teenager to her cell phone.

Addictions are harmful, perhaps overwhelmingly so—as in the cases of pornography and love addiction. . . . People may joke that they are addicted to exercise or coffee or work, and they can be. But it is only when these things seriously detract from their ability to function that people are genuinely addicted—for example, they can't stop exercising after they have suffered an injury, or they drink coffee throughout the day even though it prevents them from sleeping, or they are so preoccupied with work that they neglect their families. . . .

We all rely on fixed elements in our lives, and children especially do. It is essential to your children's security and psychological wellbeing that you provide them with consistent limits, acceptance, and love. You should also recognize that children and adolescents will often fixate on an object or activity—their stuffed animal or a recording artist, playing with dolls or video games, wearing certain clothes or going to particular places.

These fads are normal phases in growing up, and you should accept them as such.

What makes for addiction is when young people cannot extricate themselves from an activity in order to do the things required of them—things that they in some sense would *prefer* to be doing. Instead, they persist in behavior that is consistently harmful, or that is disapproved of by society, or that damages their health, their future, or their relationships with other people. . . .

Adolescent Addiction Is Not Limited to Drugs and Alcohol

Broadening our concept of addiction to include electronic devices, gambling, destructive relationships, and even eating and therapeutically prescribed drugs helps us to understand the troubling behavior of some children and adolescents.

> Alex was a normal, if quiet, child. He didn't have many friends, and from a young age preferred to spend time with electronic gadgets of various sorts. He would sit playing video games or listening to his iPod, making motions in rhythm with the music, for hours at a time.
>
> Alex did well in some school subjects—he got good grades in mathematics—and showed talent in music, which his parents encouraged. Although his father was shy and somewhat withdrawn, his mother was active and verbal and his parents' relationship was stable. Yet Alex never found a group of peers who interested him more than his electronic devices.
>
> When Alex decided not to go to college, his parents were at first shocked. But they came to accept their son's decision—not everyone is suited for college, they thought, and this might be a better path for Alex. Instead of getting out in the world, though, Alex retreated more from it. He spent all of his time alone in his room playing on his computer, listening to music, or watching television.

Alex was addicted to interacting with electronic media and entertainments. Only predictable experiences such as these made

Young people can become addicted to electronic devices, interfering with other aspects of their lives. © Alen Ajan/Flickr/Getty Images.

him feel safe and in control of his life. Alex was already isolated, and his immersion in the Internet further limited his possibility of developing a social network and outside involvements.

Alex's story suggests something remarkable—that while we are emphasizing the danger of illicit drugs and alcohol, addiction frequently emerges from ordinary aspects of children's lives. In fact, addiction may be encouraged by standard childhood and adolescent experiences—creating questions and concerns for anybody raising children today. . . .

What Causes Addiction?

Some people are more prone than others to pursue satisfaction through an external fix. "I have always been easily addicted," admitted [a] young woman . . . who sacrificed her life for a transitory love affair. Some young people turn to addictions because they can't seem to get the satisfaction they crave from their regular lives.

This susceptibility—and its opposite, resistance to addiction—stems from children's lived experiences, including their homes, neighborhoods, and school environments.

Addiction-*proof* children have:

- Skills to gain real rewards, and the patience to learn and deploy these skills
- Values that sustain moderation and reject addiction
- Confidence that they can achieve the goals and gain the rewards they desire

Addiction-*prone* children are saddled with:

- Chronic bad feelings, including fear, depression, and anxiety
- Environments that deny opportunities for fulfillment and satisfaction
- Histories of dependence, including on their parents

These personal assets don't guarantee immunity from addiction, and these deficiencies don't guarantee addiction will occur. But these addiction-preventing and -causing factors are the ones over which you have the most control. . . .

Most people—and particularly young people—leave addiction behind somewhere along their life's path. This process often involves common elements.

Young people overcome addiction when they:

- Develop the skills to gain life rewards
- Reaffirm values they have that oppose addiction
- Resolve emotional problems and become less anxious, depressed, and afraid
- Acquire assets—such as a family, work, status, security—they don't want to lose
- Mature, so that their focus shifts beyond their own needs
- Feel that they control their lives and can get what they want in the world

> "[The invalid law] abridges the First
> Amendment rights of young people
> whose parents . . . think violent video
> games are a harmless pastime."

Prohibition of the Sale of Video Games to Minors Is Unconstitutional

The Supreme Court's Decision

Antonin Scalia

In the following Supreme Court opinion, Justice Antonin Scalia explains why the Court struck down a California law prohibiting the sale of violent video games to minors. Games, like other media, are a form of free speech, he says, because they communicate ideas; and under the First Amendment, free speech cannot be restricted except for a few limitations such as obscenity. Furthermore, books and other media given to children contain just as much violence, and there is no proof that these media cause young people to commit violent acts. The fact that video games are more interactive is merely a matter of degree. Nor can a legal restriction on the sale of games to children and teens be justified as serving a need of parents, Scalia asserts, because there is already a voluntary rating

Antonin Scalia, Majority opinion, *Brown v. Entertainment Merchants Association*, US Supreme Court, June 27, 2011.

system to inform parents, and not all parents disapprove of video games.

California Assembly Bill 1179 (2005), prohibits the sale or rental of "violent video games" to minors, and requires their packaging to be labeled "18." The Act covers games "in which the range of options available to a player includes killing, maiming, dismembering, or sexually assaulting an image of a human being, if those acts are depicted" in a manner that "[a] reasonable person, considering the game as a whole, would find appeals to a deviant or morbid interest of minors," that is "patently offensive to prevailing standards in the community as to what is suitable for minors," and that "causes the game, as a whole, to lack serious literary, artistic, political, or scientific value for minors." Violation of the Act is punishable by a civil fine of up to $1,000.

Respondents, representing the video-game and software industries, brought a preenforcement challenge to the Act in the United States District Court for the Northern District of California. That court concluded that the Act violated the First Amendment and permanently enjoined its enforcement. The Court of Appeals affirmed.

Freedom of Speech Applies to New Media

California correctly acknowledges that video games qualify for First Amendment protection. The Free Speech Clause exists principally to protect discourse on public matters, but we have long recognized that it is difficult to distinguish politics from entertainment, and dangerous to try. "Everyone is familiar with instances of propaganda through fiction. What is one man's amusement, teaches another's doctrine." *Winters v. New York* (1948). Like the protected books, plays, and movies that preceded them, video games communicate ideas—and even social messages—through many familiar literary devices (such as characters, dialogue, plot, and music) and through features distinctive to the medium (such as the player's interaction with the virtual world). That suffices to confer First Amendment protection. Under our Constitution, "esthetic and moral judgments about art and literature . . . are for the individual to make, not for the Government to decree, even with the mandate or approval of a majority." *United States v. Playboy Entertainment Group* (2000). And whatever the challenges of applying the Constitution to ever-advancing technology, "the basic principles of freedom of speech and the press, like the First Amendment's command, do not vary" when a new and different medium for communication appears. *Joseph Burstyn, Inc. v. Wilson* (1952).

The most basic of those principles is this: "[A]s a general matter, . . . government has no power to restrict expression because of its message, its ideas, its subject matter, or its content." *Ashcroft v. American Civil Liberties Union* (2002). There are of course exceptions. "'From 1791 to the present,' . . . the First Amendment has 'permitted restrictions upon the content of speech in a few limited areas,' and has never 'include[d] a freedom to disregard these traditional limitations.'" *United States v. Stevens* (2010) (quoting *R.A.V. v. St. Paul* (1992)). These limited areas—such as obscenity, incitement, and fighting words—represent "well-defined and narrowly limited classes of speech, the prevention and punishment of which have never been thought to raise any Constitutional problem." . . .

Because speech about violence is not obscene, it is of no consequence that California's statute mimics the New York statute regulating obscenity-for-minors that we upheld in *Ginsberg v. New York*. That case approved a prohibition on the sale to minors of *sexual* material that would be obscene from the perspective of a child. We held that the legislature could "adjus[t] the definition of obscenity 'to social realities by permitting the appeal of this type of material to be assessed in terms of the sexual interests . . .' of . . . minors." And because "obscenity is not protected expression," the New York statute could be sustained so long as the leg-

The US Supreme Court struck down a California law banning the sale of violent video games to minors. © Joe Raedle/Getty Images News/Getty Images.

islature's judgment that the proscribed materials were harmful to children "was not irrational."

The California Act is something else entirely. It does not adjust the boundaries of an existing category of unprotected speech to ensure that a definition designed for adults is not uncritically applied to children. California does not argue that it is empowered to prohibit selling offensively violent works *to adults*—and it is wise not to, since that is but a hair's breadth from the argument rejected in *Stevens*. Instead, it wishes to create a wholly new category of content-based regulation that is permissible only for speech directed at children.

That is unprecedented and mistaken. "[M]inors are entitled to a significant measure of First Amendment protection, and only in relatively narrow and well-defined circumstances may government bar public dissemination of protected materials to them." *Erznoznik v. Jacksonville* (1975). No doubt a State possesses legitimate power to protect children from harm, but that does not include a free-floating power to restrict the ideas to which children may be exposed. "Speech that is neither obscene as to youths nor subject to some other legitimate proscription cannot be suppressed solely to protect the young from ideas or images that a legislative body thinks unsuitable for them." [*Erznoznik*].

Books Given to Children Depict Violence

California's argument would fare better if there were a longstanding tradition in this country of specially restricting children's access to depictions of violence, but there is none. Certainly the *books* we give children to read—or read to them when they are younger—contain no shortage of gore. *Grimm's Fairy Tales*, for example, are grim indeed. As her just desserts for trying to poison Snow White, the wicked queen is made to dance in red hot slippers "till she fell dead on the floor, a sad example of envy and jealousy." Cinderella's evil stepsisters have their eyes pecked out by doves. And Hansel and Gretel (children!) kill their captor by baking her in an oven.

High-school reading lists are full of similar fare. Homer's Odysseus blinds Polyphemus the Cyclops by grinding out his eye with a heated stake. In the *Inferno*, Dante and Virgil watch corrupt politicians struggle to stay submerged beneath a lake of boiling pitch, lest they be skewered by devils above the surface. And [William] Golding's *Lord of the Flies* recounts how a schoolboy called Piggy is savagely murdered *by other children* while marooned on an island.

This is not to say that minors' consumption of violent entertainment has never encountered resistance. In the 1800's, dime novels depicting crime and "penny dreadfuls" (named for their price and content) were blamed in some quarters for juvenile delinquency. When motion pictures came along, they became the villains instead. "The days when the police looked upon dime novels as the most dangerous of textbooks in the school for crime are drawing to a close. . . . They say that the moving picture machine . . . tends even more than did the dime novel to turn the thoughts of the easily influenced to paths which sometimes lead to prison." "Moving Pictures as Helps to Crime," *N.Y. Times*, Feb. 21, 1909. For a time, our Court did permit broad censorship of movies because of their capacity to be "used for evil"[*Mutual Film Corp. v. Industrial Comm'n of Ohio* (1915)], but we eventually reversed course. Radio dramas were next, and then came comic books. Many in the late 1940's and early 1950's blamed comic books for fostering a "preoccupation with violence and horror" among the young, leading to a rising juvenile crime rate. But efforts to convince Congress to restrict comic books failed. And, of course, after comic books came television and music lyrics.

California claims that video games present special problems because they are "interactive," in that the player participates in the violent action on screen and determines its outcome. The latter feature is nothing new: Since at least the publication of *The Adventures of You: Sugarcane Island* in 1969, young readers of choose-your-own-adventure stories have been able to make decisions that determine the plot by following instructions about which page to turn to. As for the argument that video games enable participation in the violent action, that seems to us more a matter of degree than of kind. As Judge [Richard] Posner has observed, all literature is interactive. "[T]he better it is, the more interactive. Literature when it is successful draws the reader into the story, makes him identify with the characters, invites him to judge them and quarrel with them, to experience their joys and sufferings as the reader's own." *American Amusement Machine Assn. v. Kendrick* [2001].

Justice [Samuel] Alito [in his concurring opinion] has done considerable independent research to identify video games in which "the violence is astounding." "Victims are dismembered, decapitated, disemboweled, set on fire, and chopped into little pieces. . . . Blood gushes, splatters, and pools." Justice Alito recounts all these disgusting video games in order to disgust us— but disgust is not a valid basis for restricting expression. And the same is true of Justice Alito's description of those video games

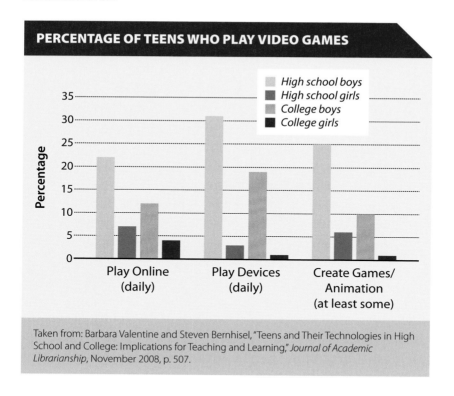

PERCENTAGE OF TEENS WHO PLAY VIDEO GAMES

Legend: High school boys, High school girls, College boys, College girls

Categories: Play Online (daily), Play Devices (daily), Create Games/Animation (at least some)

Taken from: Barbara Valentine and Steven Bernhisel, "Teens and Their Technologies in High School and College: Implications for Teaching and Learning," *Journal of Academic Librarianship*, November 2008, p. 507.

he has discovered that have a racial or ethnic motive for their violence—"'ethnic cleansing' [of] ... African Americans, Latinos, or Jews." To what end does he relate this? Does it somehow increase the "aggressiveness" that California wishes to suppress? Who knows? But it does arouse the reader's ire, and the reader's desire to put an end to this horrible message. Thus, ironically, Justice Alito's argument highlights the precise danger posed by the California Act: that the *ideas* expressed by speech—whether it be violence, or gore, or racism—and not its objective effects, may be the real reason for governmental proscription.

There Is No Proof That Violent Video Games Harm Minors

Because the Act imposes a restriction on the content of protected speech, it is invalid unless California can demonstrate that it passes strict scrutiny—that is, unless it is justified by a compelling government interest and is narrowly drawn to serve that interest. The State must specifically identify an "actual problem" in need of solving, and the curtailment of free speech must be actually necessary to the solution. That is a demanding standard. "It is rare that a regulation restricting speech because of its content will ever be permissible." [*U.S. v. Playboy*].

California cannot meet that standard. At the outset, it acknowledges that it cannot show a direct causal link between violent video games and harm to minors. Rather, relying upon our decision in *Turner Broadcasting System, Inc. v. FCC* (1994), the State claims that it need not produce such proof because the legislature can make a predictive judgment that such a link exists, based on competing psychological studies. But reliance on *Turner Broadcasting* is misplaced. That decision applied *intermediate scrutiny* to a content-neutral regulation. California's burden is much higher, and because it bears the risk of uncertainty, ambiguous proof will not suffice.

The State's evidence is not compelling. California relies primarily on the research of Dr. Craig Anderson and a few other research psychologists whose studies purport to show a connection between exposure to violent video games and harmful effects on children. These studies have been rejected by every court to consider them, and with good reason: They do not prove that violent video games *cause* minors to *act* aggressively (which would at least be a beginning). Instead, "[n]early all of the research is based on correlation, not evidence of causation, and most of the studies suffer from significant, admitted flaws in methodology." *Video Software Dealers Assn.* [*v. Schwarzenegger* (2007)]. They show at best some correlation between exposure to violent entertainment and minuscule real-world effects, such as children's feeling more aggressive or making louder noises in the few minutes after playing a violent game than after playing a nonviolent game.

Even taking for granted Dr. Anderson's conclusions that violent video games produce some effect on children's feelings

of aggression, those effects are both small and indistinguish-
able from effects produced by other media. In his testimony in a
similar lawsuit, Dr. Anderson admitted that the "effect sizes" of
children's exposure to violent video games are "about the same"
as that produced by their exposure to violence on television.
And he admits that the *same* effects have been found when children watch cartoons starring Bugs Bunny or the Road Runner,
or when they play video games like *Sonic the Hedgehog* that are
rated "E" (appropriate for all ages), or even when they "vie[w] a
picture of a gun."

Of course, California has (wisely) declined to restrict Saturday
morning cartoons, the sale of games rated for young children, or
the distribution of pictures of guns. The consequence is that its
regulation is wildly underinclusive when judged against its asserted justification, which in our view is alone enough to defeat
it. Underinclusiveness raises serious doubts about whether the
government is in fact pursuing the interest it invokes, rather than
disfavoring a particular speaker or viewpoint. Here, California
has singled out the purveyors of video games for disfavored
treatment—at least when compared to booksellers, cartoonists,
and movie producers—and has given no persuasive reason why.

Parents, Not the Law, Should Have Authority on the Restriction of Video Games

The Act is also seriously underinclusive in another respect—and
a respect that renders irrelevant the contentions of the concur-
rence and the dissents that video games are qualitatively different
from other portrayals of violence. The California Legislature is
perfectly willing to leave this dangerous, mind-altering material
in the hands of children so long as one parent (or even an aunt
or uncle) says it's OK. And there are not even any requirements
as to how this parental or avuncular relationship is to be verified;
apparently the child's or putative parent's, aunt's, or uncle's say-so
suffices. That is not how one addresses a serious social problem.

California claims that the Act is justified in aid of parental authority: By requiring that the purchase of violent video games can be made only by adults, the Act ensures that parents can decide what games are appropriate. At the outset, we note our doubts that punishing third parties for conveying protected speech to children *just in case* their parents disapprove of that speech is a proper governmental means of aiding parental authority. Accepting that position would largely vitiate the rule that "only in relatively narrow and well-defined circumstances may government bar public dissemination of protected materials to [minors]." *Erznoznik.*

But leaving that aside, California cannot show that the Act's restrictions meet a substantial need of parents who wish to restrict their children's access to violent video games but cannot do so. The video-game industry has in place a voluntary rating system designed to inform consumers about the content of games. The system, implemented by the Entertainment Software Rating Board (ESRB), assigns age-specific ratings to each video game submitted: EC (Early Childhood); E (Everyone); E10+ (Everyone 10 and older); T (Teens); M (17 and older); and AO (Adults Only—18 and older). The Video Software Dealers Association encourages retailers to prominently display information about the ESRB system in their stores; to refrain from renting or selling adults-only games to minors; and to rent or sell "M" rated games to minors only with parental consent. In 2009, the Federal Trade Commission (FTC) found that, as a result of this system, "the video game industry outpaces the movie and music industries" in "(1) restricting target-marketing of mature-rated products to children; (2) clearly and prominently disclosing rating information; and (3) restricting children's access to mature-rated products at retail." FTC, Report to Congress, Marketing Violent Entertainment to Children. This system does much to ensure that minors cannot purchase seriously violent games on their own, and that parents who care about the matter can readily evaluate the games their children bring home. Filling the remaining modest gap in concerned-parents' control can hardly be a compelling state interest.

And finally, the Act's purported aid to parental authority is vastly overinclusive. Not all of the children who are forbidden to purchase violent video games on their own have parents who *care* whether they purchase violent video games. While some of the legislation's effect may indeed be in support of what some parents of the restricted children actually want, its entire effect is only in support of what the State thinks parents *ought* to want. This is not the narrow tailoring to "assisting parents" that restriction of First Amendment rights requires.

Legal Banning of Video Games Abridges the Rights of Young People

California's effort to regulate violent video games is the latest episode in a long series of failed attempts to censor violent entertainment for minors. While we have pointed out above that some of the evidence brought forward to support the harmfulness of video games is unpersuasive, we do not mean to demean or disparage the concerns that underlie the attempt to regulate them— concerns that may and doubtless do prompt a good deal of parental oversight. We have no business passing judgment on the view of the California Legislature that violent video games (or, for that matter, any other forms of speech) corrupt the young or harm their moral development. Our task is only to say whether or not such works constitute a "well-defined and narrowly limited clas[s] of speech, the prevention and punishment of which have never been thought to raise any Constitutional problem" [*Chaplinsky v. New Hampshire* (1942)] (the answer plainly is no); and if not, whether the regulation of such works is justified by that high degree of necessity we have described as a compelling state interest (it is not). Even where the protection of children is the object, the constitutional limits on governmental action apply.

The Dissenting Opinion of Justice Stephen Breyer

California's statute . . . imposes a restriction on speech that is modest at most. That restriction is justified by a compelling interest (supplementing parents' efforts to prevent their children from purchasing potentially harmful violent, interactive material). And there is no equally effective, less restrictive alternative. California's statute is consequently constitutional on its face—though litigants remain free to challenge the statute as applied in particular instances, including any effort by the State to apply it to minors aged 17. I add that the majority's different conclusion creates a serious anomaly in First Amendment law. *Ginsberg* [*v. New York*] makes clear that a State can prohibit the sale to minors of depictions of nudity; today the Court makes clear that a State cannot prohibit the sale to minors of the most violent interactive video games. But what sense does it make to forbid selling to a 13-year-old boy a magazine with an image of a nude woman, while protecting a sale to that 13-year-old of an interactive video game in which he actively, but virtually, binds and gags the woman, then tortures and kills her? What kind of First Amendment would permit the government to protect children by restricting sales of that extremely violent video game *only* when the woman—bound, gagged, tortured, and killed—is also topless? . . .

This case is ultimately less about censorship than it is about education. Our Constitution cannot succeed in securing the liberties it seeks to protect unless we can raise future generations committed cooperatively to making our system of government work. Education, however, is about choices. Sometimes, children need to learn by making choices for themselves. Other times, choices are made for children—by their parents, by their teachers, and by the people acting democratically through their governments. In my view, the First Amendment does not disable government from helping parents make such a choice here.

Stephen Breyer, dissenting opinion, Brown v.
Entertainment Merchants Association,
US Supreme Court, June 27, 2011.

California's legislation straddles the fence between (1) addressing a serious social problem and (2) helping concerned parents control their children. Both ends are legitimate, but when they affect First Amendment rights they must be pursued by means that are neither seriously underinclusive nor seriously overinclusive. As a means of protecting children from portrayals of violence, the legislation is seriously underinclusive, not only because it excludes portrayals other than video games, but also because it permits a parental or avuncular veto. And as a means of assisting concerned parents it is seriously overinclusive because it abridges the First Amendment rights of young people whose parents (and aunts and uncles) think violent video games are a harmless pastime. And the overbreadth in achieving one goal is not cured by the underbreadth in achieving the other. Legislation such as this, which is neither fish nor fowl, cannot survive strict scrutiny.

> "I watched and worried as our media began to function as a force field separating my children from what my son, only half-ironically, called RL (Real Life)."

A Mother Relates Her Decision to Impose an Electronic Media Ban at Home

Personal Narrative

Susan Maushart

In the following viewpoint, Susan Maushart, a columnist and author who lives in Australia, describes how and why she and her teenage children stopped using electronic media for six months, an experiment she has described at length in her book The Winter of Our Disconnect. *The teens could not remember a time before computers and cell phones were central in people's lives, and even she had become excessively dependent on electronic media. Although she believes technology enhances life, she wanted to find out whether there might be too much reliance on it. She decided that the only way to do that was to conduct a personal test. Doing without media devices changed their daily life, she says, and made a great improvement on their family.*

Raising three teenagers as a single parent is no Contiki Cruise at the best of times. But when I decided we should all set sail for a six-month screen-free adventure, it suddenly came closer to *The Caine Mutiny*, with me in the Bogart role.

There were lots of reasons why we pulled the plug on our electronic media . . . or, I should say, why I did, because heaven knows my children would have sooner volunteered to go without food, water or hair products. At ages 14, 15 and 18, my daughters and my son don't use media. They inhabit media. And they do so exactly as fish inhabit a pond. Gracefully. Unblinkingly. And utterly without consciousness or curiosity as to how they got there.

They don't remember a time before email, or instant messaging, or Google. Even the media of their own childhood—VHS and dial-up, Nintendo 64 and "cordful" phones—they regard as relics, as quaint as inkwells.

They collectively refer to civilisation pre-high-definition flatscreen as "the black and white days".

My kids—like yours, I'm guessing—are part of a generation that cut its teeth, literally and figuratively, on a keyboard, learning to say "'puter" along with "mama", "juice" and "now!" They're kids who have had cellphones and wireless internet longer than they've had molars. Who multi-task their schoolwork alongside five or six other electronic inputs, to the syncopated beat of the Instant Messenger pulsing insistently like some distant tribal tom-tom.

Wait a minute. Did I say they do their schoolwork like that? Correction. They do their life like that.

When my children laugh, they don't say "ha ha", they say "LOL". In fact, they conjugate it. ("LOL at this picture before I Photoshopped your nose, Mum!")

They download movies and TV shows as casually as you or I might switch on the radio. And when I remind them piracy is a crime, they look at one another and go "LOL". These are kids who shrug when they lose their iPods, with all 5000 tunes and Lord-knows-what in the way of video clips, feature films and "TV" shows (like, who watches TV on a television anymore?). "There's plenty more where that came from", their attitude says.

And the most infuriating thing of all? They're right. The digital content that powers their world, like matter itself, can never truly be destroyed. Like the Magic Pudding of Australian legend, it's a dessert bar that never runs out of cheesecake.

There's so much that's wonderful, and at the same time nauseating, about that.

The Experiment

The Winter of Our Disconnect—aka The Experiment (as we all eventually came to call it)—was in some ways an accident waiting to happen. Over a period of years, I watched and worried as our media began to function as a force field separating my children from what my son, only half-ironically, called RL (Real Life). But, to be honest, the teenagers weren't the only ones with dependency issues.

Although a relatively recent arrival to the global village, I'd been known to abuse information too. (Sneaking my iPhone into the toilet? Did I have no self-respect?) As a journalist, it was easy to hide my habit, but deep down I knew I was hooked.

The Winter of Our Disconnect started out as a kind of purge. It ended up as so much more. Long story short: our digital detox messed with our heads, our hearts and our homework. It changed the way we ate and the way we slept, the way we "friended", fought, planned and played. It altered the very taste and texture of our family life. Hell, it even altered the mouth-feel.

In the end, our family's self-imposed exile from the Information Age changed our lives indelibly—and infinitely for the better.

At the simplest level, *The Winter of Our Disconnect* is the story of how one highly idiosyncratic family survived six months of wandering through the desert, digitally speaking, and the lessons we learned about ourselves and our technology along the way. At the same time, our story is a channel to a wider view into the impact of new media on the lives of families, into the very heart of the meaning of home.

"Only connect", implored EM Forster in his acclaimed novel *Howard's End,* published a century ago.

Ninety-nine years and one trillion web pages later, "only connect" is a goal we have achieved with a vengeance. So much so that our biggest challenge today may be finding the moral courage to log off.

Today, some 93 per cent of teenagers are online. Three-quarters own an iPod or MP3 player, 60 per cent have their own computer and 71 per cent a cellphone, according to figures from the 2007 Pew Internet & American Life Project. But the most provocative statistics are those that show how intensely our children interact with their media.

In a large-scale study of young people who use media, conducted in 2005—ancient history already—up to a third told the US-based Kaiser Family Foundation they were using multiple electronic devices simultaneously "most of the time".

An average American teenager spends 8½ hours a day in some form of mass-mediated interaction. That's more time than he or she will spend doing anything else, including sleeping. Because media use in families is directly correlated with income, the figures are higher still in households at the more affluent end of the socio-economic spectrum, and where parents are more highly educated.

Excessive Media Use?

For Generation M, as the Kaiser report dubbed these 8–18-year-olds, media use is not an activity, it's an environment: pervasive, invisible, shrink-wrapped around pretty much everything kids do and say and think. How adaptive an environment is the question—and the answer, not surprisingly, seems to depend entirely on whom you ask.

The Pew Project found that, among teens, 88 per cent are convinced that technology makes their lives easier. A decidedly more ambivalent 69 per cent of parents say the same—although two-thirds also make some effort to regulate their children's use of media in some way (rules about safe sites, file sharing, time use, etc.).

Yet an astonishing 30 per cent of parents believe media has no effect on their children one way or the other.

Maybe that's wishful thinking. On the other hand, maybe it's not wishful enough.

I happen to believe that the possibilities held out to us by media are hugely exciting. I am not a Golden-Ager, lamenting the decline of the candle in a neon-lit world. Not in the least. I love my gadgets. I think my life is enhanced by technology. And I know the world at large is.

Yet the idea that there might be a media equivalent of what micro-finance guru David Bussau calls "an economics of enough" continued to occupy my thoughts.

It was an intriguing set of questions, but how could I test my hypotheses/hunches?

That's when I remembered Barry Marshall—the Australian microbiologist who won a Nobel Prize in 2005 for the simple but astounding discovery that stomach ulcers are caused by bacteria. Not stress, or spicy foods, or excess acid. Germs. Plain old germs. In retrospect, it seems so obvious. In the early '80s, Marshall's theory was dismissed as outlandish—especially by the pharmaceutical companies that underwrite the clinical trials by which medical research is tested. Frustrated but undaunted, Marshall decided to take matters into his own hands . . . indeed, into his own stomach lining. He swallowed some of the bacteria in question and waited to see whether he would develop an ulcer. He did. And the rest—give or take a decade of intensive further research—is history

So it occurred to me: if Marshall could use his own life as a petri dish, why couldn't I? (Gulp.)

> *"Texting, Facebook and video games are not inherently bad. Nor are they inherently better or worse than watching TV."*

Teens' Use of Electronic Devices Does No More Harm than TV

Beth J. Harpaz

In the following viewpoint, Beth J. Harpaz, an award-winning writer for the Associated Press and the author of several books, reports that although it is often said that teenagers spend too much time texting, using Facebook, and playing video games, some experts question whether this is any worse than the hours today's parents spent watching television when they were teens. Research has shown that excessive time devoted to electronic media correlates with poor grades in school, but one psychologist points out that once students have finished their homework, screen time in itself does not matter. Some parents have found that not resisting today's communication trends leads to happier family life.

Let's face it: Teenagers spend hours texting, socializing on Facebook and playing video games. And it's driving their parents nuts.

Sure, there are real dangers associated with all this screen time—everything from cyberbullying to couch-potato obesity. Not to mention driving while texting, shortened attention spans and Internet porn.

But many of today's parents spent hours as kids sitting in front of screens too—only they were TV screens.

Which raises an interesting question: Is Facebook really worse for teenagers' brains than the mindless reruns of *Gilligan's Island* and *The Brady Bunch* that their parents consumed growing up?

Douglas Gentile, a child psychologist and associate professor at Iowa State University in Ames, Iowa, who studies the effects of media on children, says texting, Facebook and video games are not inherently bad. Nor are they inherently better or worse than watching TV, although they do pose different risks, such as cyberbullying.

But research has shown that the more time kids spend in front of screens—whether it's TV or instant-messaging—the worse their school performance. "That doesn't mean it's true for every kid, but it makes sense, that for every hour a kid is playing video games, it's an hour that they're not doing homework or reading or exploring or creating," he said.

Gentile calls this the "displacement hypothesis. If screen time is displacing doing their homework, that's bad. But if their homework is done, well, so what?"

Gentile, who admits that his own teenager crossed the "9,000 texts in one month barrier" last summer, acknowledged that parents are struggling to adjust to a world in which kids would rather look at words on a cellphone screen than have a conversation.

"The older generation, it's not their culture," he said. "There is a resistance to it."

Resistant to Change

Watching TV as a family, as mindless as that experience can be, is now regarded with nostalgia by parents. If your kid is sitting in the living room watching *American Idol*, you can plop on the sofa with them, and "it's a shared experience," Gentile said. But if they're texting or video-chatting with a friend from school, "it's a private experience. It's like they're whispering secrets. And we find it rude."

Patti Rowlson, a mother of two in Everson, Wash., says this "has been a topic of discussion in our house for years now." She and her husband started out limiting TV time when their kids were little, but "then technology crept in. Cellphones, laptop computers, iPods with Wi-Fi. We, as parents, were no longer in control of screen time because we could not even tell when they were using it."

Recounting a struggle that will sound familiar to many parents, Rowlson said that at first, she and her husband imposed limits on tech use.

"There were battles and even groundings," along with the confiscation of iPods, she said. "We were constantly policing and the kids were constantly getting in trouble. We were trying to fight for the old ways, and it was causing a lot of stress and tension in the family. It was ridiculous. So we loosened up. And it's made everybody happier. We were fighting something that you can't hold back. It's how they communicate with their peers."

What's been the result? Two good kids, she said. "In the end I'm not sure if having boundaries early on helped them or made no difference at all."

Ron Neal, who lives in West L.A., has a teenage daughter who is "tech-driven and passionate about it. . . . I don't know how it's going to play out, but I don't have this fear and dread about it."

Neal, who admits to watching a lot of *Gilligan's Island* growing up, added: "We had our minds numbed by TV, and maybe they're looking at useless things on the Internet or YouTube, but

Some experts warn that multitasking with different electronic devices leads to poor performance. © E. Jason Wambsgans/Chicago Tribune/MCT via Getty Images.

I also think they're developing a lot of skills through this technology that we could never comprehend. For my daughter, when she is home, she does have everything going—the TV, the computer, communicating with friends, and doing the homework at the same time."

He admits, though, that there are some frightening aspects to the dependence today's teenagers have on technology. "They are so emotionally connected to being tied in with their friends 24 hours a day, if they get a text, they feel obligated to respond in seconds," he said. He recalled a group of girls showing up for a birthday party at a restaurant, and "every one of them had their head down, texting."

Impact of Screen Time

The explosion in teen screen time is well-documented. A recent Associated Press-mtvU poll found that one-third of college students use computers, cellphones or gaming consoles for six or

"How are you ever going to text," by Dave Carpenter. www.CartoonStock.com. Copyright © Dave Carpenter. Reproduction rights obtainable from www.CartoonStock.com.

more hours daily. A Kaiser Family Foundation study published in January [2010] found that total media use among 8- to 18-year-olds, including TV, music, computers, video games, print and movies, has increased from six hours, 21 minutes daily in 2004 to seven hours, 38 minutes in 2009.

"Try waking a teenager in the morning and the odds are good that you'll find a cellphone tucked under their pillow," the Kaiser report said.

The Kaiser study also found that the more time kids spend with media, the lower their grades and levels of personal contentment are.

Gentile said the impact of screen time on school work can be mitigated by what he calls "protective factors." Those might include good teachers and a high-performing school, love of reading, coming from a family where education is valued, and exposure to experiences that are culturally and intellectually enriching. "If you had all these protective factors," said Gentile, "then that one little risk factor (screen time), who cares?"

He added that surprisingly, the amount of time kids spend watching TV has not declined precipitously with the popularity of computers and gaming, but "they don't pay nearly the attention (to TV) that they used to." The TV might be on, but "they're also instant-messaging, they're on Facebook, they're texting."

One thing parents should worry about, Gentile said, is the way electronic devices encourage multitasking.

"Multitasking is not really good for anyone," he said. "Your reflexes speed up, you're quicker to look over your shoulder and notice little noises or lights. This is not what they need when they get to the classroom and you're supposed to ignore the kid next to you. Scanning to see when the next message comes, this may not be good for kids. The more distractions you have, the worse your performance is." Getting kids to turn off their phones, iPods, and computers in order to concentrate on homework and reading, he said, "I think that's a fight worth having."

Bottom line: Never mind that your kid is spending two hours on Facebook each night. As long as they do their homework without texting in between math problems, it's probably no better or worse than the hours you spent watching *Star Trek*.

> *"Nearly 65% of teens at 'no phone'*
> *schools bring their cell phone to school*
> *every day, anyway."*

Many Teens Ignore School Cell Phone Regulations

Amanda Lenhart et al.

In the following viewpoint, Amanda Lenhart, the director of the Pew Internet & American Life Project's research on teens, children, and families, discusses the use of cell phones in schools. Most schools view them as disruptive if used in the classroom, she says, and many take them away from students who are caught, but this policy is not consistently enforced. Two-thirds of students report they have sent or received text messages in class despite the rule against it. About 25 percent have made occasional phone calls during class. Only 17 percent of students at schools that forbid possession of cell phones on campus have never brought their phone to school.

As institutions that are often called upon to serve *in loco parentis* [in place of parents], schools take a variety of approaches towards the regulation of the mobile phone within their four walls and on their campuses.

When it comes to possession of a mobile phone during the school day, just 12% of teens with cell phones say that they can have a cell phone at their school at all times. A majority of teens (62%) say that they can have a cell phone at school but not in class, and another quarter of teens (24%) attend schools that forbid cell phones altogether.

Our focus group conversations support these findings and suggest that most schools treat phones as a disruptive force to be kept turned off and away from the classroom. Many teens talked about a tiered system based on a "if they can see it, they can take it" philosophy. An older high school girl describes a common system: "Yeah, it's happened to me three times. The first time they take it for a day. They take it for a night and you don't see it until the end of the next day of school. The second time they take it for a week, and the third time the rest of the semester." Other teens describe systems in schools that require parents to come to the school to retrieve the phones of wayward students.

Some schools allow limited use of cell phones, as this older high school girl explains, "At ours, you can have it in passing periods and lunch. And if they see it, it gets taken and I think the first time you go back at the end of the day and get it."

Arbitrary Enforcement

Some teens describe what feels like arbitrary enforcement or a lack of clarity around school rules for mobile phones. "Our rules are just like whatever the teacher feels like," said one younger high school-age boy. "Some teachers give [the phone back] to you at the end of the day, some after class, some keep it over the weekend if it's like, Thursday or Friday." Others described schools "giving seniors leeway" with phones and teachers playing favorites or looking the other way around cell phone enforcement. Said one middle school girl, "At my school, it's kind of messed up, but if you're one of the favorites, and I'm one of the favorites with some of my teachers, they just let you use your phone."

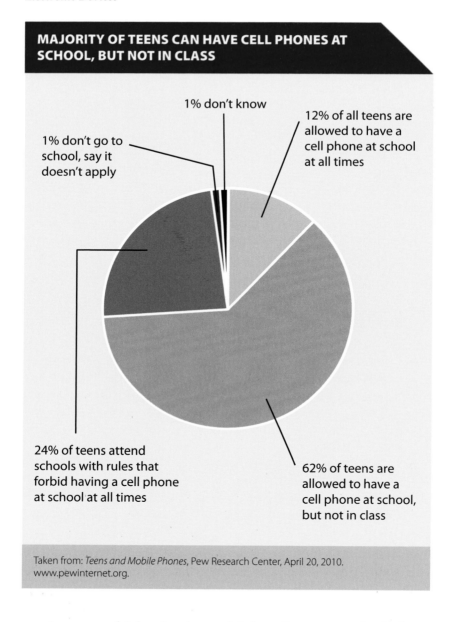

MAJORITY OF TEENS CAN HAVE CELL PHONES AT SCHOOL, BUT NOT IN CLASS

1% don't know

1% don't go to school, say it doesn't apply

12% of all teens are allowed to have a cell phone at school at all times

24% of teens attend schools with rules that forbid having a cell phone at school at all times

62% of teens are allowed to have a cell phone at school, but not in class

Taken from: *Teens and Mobile Phones*, Pew Research Center, April 20, 2010. www.pewinternet.org.

A younger high school-age girl describes one teacher's classroom policy: "Well, my teacher has a mind of her own, so she takes up the phones in class before class starts and then at the end she'll give them back. That's just her policy, but if you don't turn it in and it goes off, then it gets sent to the principal and your parents have to come pick it up." Another high school-age girl describes a creative teacher, who, "if she caught you texting, she'd pick up your phone in class and read the message." This is apparently an effective deterrent according to reports of teens in our focus groups.

Other teens report that their teachers use their own phones in class: "Well, it says in the book that you're not supposed to have it, like if you have it, it's supposed to be off and in your book bag or whatever, but like it's extremely flexible. Like, some of my teachers even use their phone in class, so you can use it as long as it doesn't make noise."

A few schools simply ban phones altogether: "We have absolutely no cell phones," said one older high school girl. "If you're on school grounds, you can't even use it in your car."

Despite these restrictions, teens are still overwhelmingly taking their phones to school—77% take their phones with them to school every school day and another 7% take their phone to school at least several times a week. Less than 10% of teens take their phone to school less often and just 8% say they never take their phone to school.

While a higher percentage of teens who attend schools that forbid all cell phones say they never bring their phone to school (17% vs. 5% at other schools), nearly 65% of teens at "no phone" schools bring their cell phone to school every day, anyway. Four in five (81%) teens at schools where they may have a cell phone, just not in class, bring their phone to school everyday.

Further, many teens who take their phones to school are keeping them on and using them during the school day, sometimes during instructional time. Six in ten teens (60%) say they have their phone turned on at school at least once a day and sometimes several times a day. Just one-quarter of teens (23%) who take their phones to school say they never have them turned on during the school day.

Teens with carte blanche to have their phone with them at school are just as likely as teens who can have the phone, just not in class, to have their phone on several times during the school day. Some 49% of both groups report such behavior. Teens who are not allowed to have a phone at school are more likely to say they keep the phone off during the school day, with one-third (32%) saying they never turn their phones on, compared with 21% of teens who can have phones at school but not in class, and 16% of teens who have fewer restrictions.

Texting During Class

More striking is the two-thirds of teens (64%) who tote their phones to school who say they have ever sent or received a text message during class. Nearly one-third (31%) of teens who take their phones to school text in class several times a day and another 12% of those teens say they text in class at least once a day. Fewer teens report that they place calls during class, though 4% manage to make calls from class several times a day and another 4% do so at least once a day. Fully 75% of teens who bring their phones to school say they never make calls during class time.

One middle school boy describes texting in class at his school: "When I'm in class, I just see people pull out their phone and try to be sneaky, and get past the teachers and try texting and stuff. Like, one time I tried that and my teacher caught me."

Teens in the focus groups described a myriad of ways to text in class without being caught—behind stacks of books, under desktops, inside of bags, and one even described having an older phone that he kept in his bag to surrender to teachers when he got caught texting in class. "I've got [a second phone] . . . if you get caught using your phone you can pull out a fake phone, turn it on and give it to them."

In-class texting varies little with regard to the aggressiveness of a school's regulation of its students' mobile phones—teens with full access to cell phones are just a bit more likely (71% to 58%) to say they send or receive texts in class than teens who

Teens commonly ignore bans on cell phone use in school. © Hill Street Studios/Blend Images/ Getty Images.

attend schools that forbid phones altogether. Perhaps heartening to administrators is the finding that about a third of teens text frequently in class (31%), another third of teens (33%) text in class occasionally and a third (36%) say they never send text messages during class. These findings mostly hold regardless of the regulatory environment, although there are exceptions in the extremes of behavior. Teens in schools where phones are totally forbidden are slightly less likely to text in class several times a day, and are more likely to say they never text, than are teens who attend schools that allow cell phones at all times.

Roughly 25% of teens take their cell phones to school and say they have made a phone call on their cell phone during class, although most do so only infrequently. The data show that 13% of teens who bring their cell phones to school make a cell call during class less often than once a week and just 4% make such calls several times a week. Another 4% say they make calls at least once a day and yet another 4% say they make calls several times a day during class. There are few statistically significant differences on this question by school regulatory environment.

Girls and older teens are more likely than boys and younger teens to take their cell phones to school every day. Teens from lower income families are more likely to say that they make calls during class time several times a day, with 12% of teens whose parents earn less than $30,000 annually saying they make calls that frequently compared with just 2% of teens from wealthier families.

> *"I can't recall a single class I've ever had that's been seriously disrupted by inter-student telephonic communications."*

A Student Asserts That Texting in Class Is Not Disruptive

Personal Narrative

Alex Howard

In the following viewpoint, Alex Howard, editor-in-chief of the student newspaper of North Eugene High School in Eugene, Oregon, says that he has never been in a class that was disrupted by students texting in class. The only disruptions have been caused by teachers' reactions to it. He feels that this causes a distraction from classwork, and that the policy forbidding texting should be critically evaluated. Phone calls during class should be banned, he says, but not texting. Though some people argue that texting keeps students from concentrating on their work, he considers it less of a problem than doing homework in class, which is allowed. In his opinion the ban is outdated, ill-conceived, and technophobic.

I think it's pretty fair to say we're all horribly familiar with the mantra by now. "*No phones in class, please.*" "*You can have*

*your phone back after school." "I SAID GIVE ME YOUR PHONE,
YOU TWISTED LITTLE SNOT!"*[1] Not a day goes by when I don't
hear somebody complained at for using their phone during class,
something I'm sure my fellow students can agree with. It's so
routine, so unremarkable, that nobody thinks about it anymore.
That's not to say we don't text in class, of course; we just make
sure we're much more discreet about it. I myself am no stranger
to such clandestine communications—honestly, who is?

Which raises a rather obvious question. I can't recall a single
class I've ever had that's been seriously disrupted by inter-student
telephonic communications. In fact, the only disruptions of note
are caused by teachers themselves, reacting to students texting,
Facebooking, or what have you. Many times I've seen my teachers
interrupt themselves to snap a few harsh words at somebody . . .
ordering them to put their phone away, and providing other students with a momentary target of derision. This serves to do little
more than distract other students and has been known on occasion to knock the entire class off topic for significant periods
of time—and for what? To shame another student who had the
temerity to spend a few moments multi-tasking with something
not related to the class?

And what does it accomplish? Usually, the student chewed
out for their ostensibly offensive behavior just returns their attention to their phone as soon as the teacher turns their gaze elsewhere, feeling slightly more animosity towards their teacher than
they might have otherwise. I mean no disrespect to the dedicated,
hard-working, eminently capable staff of North Eugene when I
say this, but dealing with phone use in class has become a protocol
inculcated by habit to the point where it is almost a religious pre-
cept: *phones shouldn't be used in class; don't try to think about it ra-
tionally, just apply the policy. Do not question the Party. Big Brother
is watching.* Yet evaluating North's cell phone policy critically—as
all policies *should* be evaluated—reveals a clearly well-intentioned
but woefully thought-out system. Instead of helping students to
pay attention in class by punishing cell phone use, teachers are

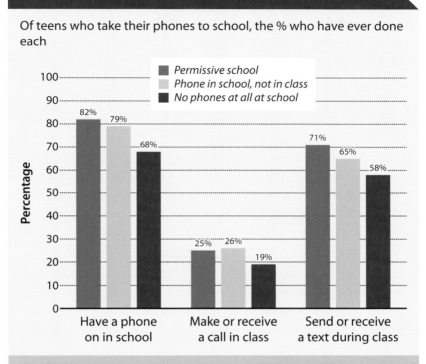

PERCENTAGE OF TEENS WHO SEND TEXT MESSAGES IN CLASS

Of teens who take their phones to school, the % who have ever done each

Legend:
- Permissive school
- Phone in school, not in class
- No phones at all at school

Have a phone on in school: 82%, 79%, 68%
Make or receive a call in class: 25%, 26%, 19%
Send or receive a text during class: 71%, 65%, 58%

(Y-axis: Percentage, 0 to 100)

Taken from: *Teens and Mobile Phones*, Pew Research Center, April 20, 2010. www.pewinternet.org.

themselves causing disruptions in trying to enforce anti-cell-phone policies. This surely cannot be a desirable result.

Ban Phone Calls, Not Texting

This is not to say, of course, that cell phone use should be unrestricted and unequivocally permitted. I think it's entirely fair to ban phone calls in class; they're genuinely disruptive and obnoxious, and are detrimental to a positive learning environment. But should teachers really be smacking down on *all* cell phone use, regardless of whether it's disruptive?

One could reasonably argue that cell phone use isn't just a matter of disrupting class, it's a matter of impeding individual learning. It distracts students from the topic at hand and might hinder their ability to perform well in the class. I'd disagree with this slightly—briefly answering a text message is much less distracting than, say, doing homework during class time, something very few teachers prohibit. And investigation of my own has revealed that it's pretty clear that personal distraction is not the motivation for teachers to intervene. In one of my classes—one I selected specifically . . . for the teacher's particular intolerance of cell phones—I spent most of an entire lecture doodling on an old assignment and looking for all the world like I was ignoring every word the teacher said, quite without any attempts on behalf of the teacher to regain my attention.

In the end, one can only conclude that cell phone bans are little more than an outdated, ill-conceived, and technophobic habit ingrained in the minds of both students and teachers to the point where they aren't questioned. And lack of questioning is lack of thought—precisely the opposite of what should be promoted in schools.

Note

1. Disclaimer: I have never actually heard a teacher call a student a "twisted little snot." Not yet, anyway. I can wait.

"Teachers . . . are finding that having students text answers to questions via websites allows them an on-the-spot gauge of student understanding."

Some Schools Encourage Using Cell Phones as Classroom Tools

Colleen Gillard

In the following viewpoint, Colleen Gillard, an education writer based in Massachusetts, reports that in some schools, students are asked to use their cell phones in class to complete assignments. Because most teens already have phones but some do not have computers at home, this policy is useful to teachers whose schools lack the funds to provide classroom computers, and it encourages students to write. Phones are used to upload texts to class blogs and to answer quizzes via websites, providing both students and teachers with instant feedback. Assignments are limited to tasks that can be done with the simplest cell phones because many students cannot afford smartphones, but a poll has found that a majority of teens prefer smartphones to laptops, and in the future their use may be expanded.

In Santa Ana, Calif., Judy Pederson smiles when she sees her ninth-grade English Literature class bent over their cell phones, furiously texting. They are engaged and on task, and she will soon have their thoughts on the possible consequences of Friar Lawrence marrying two star-crossed lovers in sixteenth-century Verona. The students' texts go from their phones to a website to the white board on her classroom wall.

"Before, it was difficult getting them to write," says the Valley High School teacher, who has decided to exploit rather than fight the oft-observed teen addiction to cell phones. "But now when I ask them to compose back stories or give advice to conflicted literary characters, they're into it." Her only requirement is that her students, who generally come from first-generation immigrant homes, use standard English.

Only four years ago [in 2006], 19 percent of computing devices in K–12 schools were mobile devices, according to the report *America's Digital Schools 2006*. That number has increased to 57 percent, according to a national survey of nearly 1,000 school principals and technology coordinators to be released in September by the research group Project RED. Cell phone ownership among students has increased as well. According to a 2010 Kaiser Family Foundation study, 85 percent of high school students, 69 percent of middle school students, and 31 percent of eight- to ten-year-olds now own cell phones.

Seizing on What Kids Have

For educators concerned with the digital divide, or with their districts' ability to afford technology upgrades, the popularity of cell phones among students has come as an unexpected resource arriving in their classroom. "The beauty of cell phones is that you don't need a certain demographic; all kids have them," says Liz Kolb, a University of Michigan education instructor, who wrote the 2008 book *Toys to Tools: Connecting Student Cell Phones to Education*. Kolb is a proponent of teaching with the plainest tech

Websites such as PollEverywhere.com allow students to use their cell phone for pretests. © AP Images/Quad-City Times, Larry Fisher.

device in mind. "You focus on what [most] kids have at the moment," she says.

When Pederson discovered that many of her students did not have computers or Internet access at home, and yet 88 percent had cell phones, she realized she was onto something. Having her students use their phones for in-class activities meant simply organizing them in groups to cover those without, and ensuring that homework assignments included technology-free options.

She focused her lessons around the capabilities of the dumbest phone—not too great a handicap since even the plainest phones could access websites through simple calls or texts, and download podcasts or other content. Blog sites have also made such actions as the posting of texts or recorded material onto class or individual blogs easy.

A Tool for Teachers, Too

Teachers, in turn, are finding that having students text answers to questions via websites allows them an on-the-spot gauge of student understanding. For such quick assessments, many teachers use the free Web tool www.polleverywhere.com to get instant feedback from short multiple-choice tests as well as from responses to more open-ended questions. The website enables teachers to post or graph student answers on electronic whiteboards in real time—fast results that both students and teachers like.

Jimbo Lamb, who teaches math at Annville-Cleona High School in rural, central Pennsylvania, uses www.polleverywhere.com to let him know when to move on to the next lesson. "With many students too shy to admit what they don't understand, it's always difficult to get a clear sense how a lesson is going. But with a tool that enables student anonymity, I get a quick and accurate picture."

Making use of cell phones in the classroom—rather than banning them—creates an opportunity to structure their use in a positive way, and to talk about cyberbullying and other inappropriate uses of the technology, teachers say. Judy Pederson believes that having students help compose classroom rules for cell phone use encourages compliance. In her classroom, cell phones that aren't put away when not being used are confiscated until a parent can come to retrieve them. Kolb advises teachers to ask students to leave their cell phones at the front of the room until needed for classroom activities.

Smartphones May Be Next

Meanwhile, pressure to expand cell phone use in the classroom continues to come from the kids. After New Milford (NJ) High School principal Eric Sheninger bought his staff an iPod cart with 28 iPods and an iMac computer for downloading curriculum-enrichment materials from the Web—he was chagrined to hear from students that they would have preferred smart phones instead. Smart phones comprise only two percent of mobile devices used in schools, according to the Project RED survey, but their presence is projected to increase in the near future. Since smart phones require Internet data plans, which currently cost around 30 dollars a month per phone (in addition to flat usage fees), they represent a sustained investment few schools can afford.

Nonetheless teens keep asking—something Shawn Gross, managing director of Digital Millennial Consulting, learned in 2006 when his educational-technology advisory group teamed up with the U.S. Department of Education to survey 300 disengaged students in the Washington, DC, metro area about how technology could improve the teenagers' interest in and understanding of math and science. Students told researchers that they learned best when collaborating with peers and, when asked to name their choice of technological learning tools, overwhelmingly chose smart phones over fancy new laptops. Students complained about the "hassle" posed by laptops: having to retrieve them from backpacks, finding somewhere to open them, and then waiting as they boot up. "Teenagers today want instant and continuous access to the Web," Gross says.

"Take out your phones. Open the American History app and turn to the page about George Washington."

"Take out your phones, open the American History app and turn to the page about George Washington," cartoon by Aaron Bacall. www.CartoonStock.com. Copyright © Aaron Bacall. Reproduction rights obtainable from www.CartoonStock.com.

The research team heard, but wanted to see if such complaints held up across socioeconomic and regional differences. Gross partnered with an educational nonprofit, Project Tomorrow, to ask a national sample of 350,000 students for their learning-tool preference. They received the same response: a clear majority favored smart phones over any other technology, including laptops. "The critical factors for these kids seemed to be instant, continuous access to the Internet; easy, immediate access to the device; and quick, simple contact with their peers," Gross says.

For the time being, not a lot of schools are pursuing the smartphone route unless it is with outside funding. But over time, if fees come down, Gross notes, schools may be seeing more and more students show up in class with parent-financed devices.

| "Didn't think that texting and driving
  could land you in jail? Think again."

Texting While Driving
Can Lead to Prison

Michael Pines

In the following viewpoint, Michael Pines, an attorney who represents people who have been injured in automobile accidents, describes ten of the worst cell-phone-related accidents in which people have been killed. In many of these cases, the person responsible has been sentenced to jail or prison time. A twenty-two-year-old driver who was deleting text messages when he caused the death of two teenage girls received a seven-year sentence, and an eighteen-year-old girl whose texting resulted in the death of an elderly woman will serve up to ten years in prison for vehicular homicide.

We all know that texting, talking and surfing the web are dangerous when done behind the wheel; but how often does that stop us from glancing at our phones at a red light? The truth is, distracted driving accounts for a significant percentage

Michael Pines, "Top 10 Worst Cell-Phone Related Injury Accidents of All Time: Prison Edition," Seriousaccidents.com, March 2, 2011. http://seriousaccidents.com/blog/accident -prevention/ten-worst-cell-phone-related-injuries-deaths. Reprinted by permission of Michael Pines, Law Offices of Michael Pines.

A driver is ticketed for using his cell phone while driving. © AP Images/Las Cruces Sun-News, Norm Dettlaff.

of injury accidents each year—and cell phones are one of the biggest culprits when it comes to inattentive driving.

Didn't think that texting and driving could land you in jail? Think again. We bring you the top 10 worst cell phone accidents in history, many of which have landed the violators in none other than prison.

Stay safe and out of jail: don't use your cell phone while driving.

10. *Alleged texting causes death of 5 high school cheerleaders.* In 2007, five high school cheerleaders from western New York were killed in a head-on collision with a tractor trailer. Moments before the fatal car accident, text messages were sent from and received by the teen driver's cell phone. Investigators have no way of knowing whether or not Bailey Goodman, the young woman driving at the time of the crash, was in fact responsible for the messages sent from her phone. However, AAA spokesman Michael Pina told ABC News that texting while driving is one of the

most dangerous distractions for any driver, regardless of age or driving experience.

9. *Pregnant Florida woman killed by texting driver.* Chelsea Murphy, a 19-year-old mother-to-be from Naples, Florida, was killed in a tragic car accident when she was hit by a driver using a cell phone to send text messages in March of 2010. Chelsea's mother, Kris Murphy, is now campaigning to have schools speak to students about the severe dangers of texting and driving. The *Naples News* reported that Florida has yet to institute a ban on distracted driving hazards like texting, despite Murphy's activism and that of other concerned citizens.

8. *Metrolink engineer's texting activity ends in deadly commuter crash.* In September of 2008, a California Metrolink train carrying commuters through the San Fernando Valley collided with a freight train, killing 25 people and injuring an additional 135 passengers. The engineer responsible for directing the train was texting with a teenage train enthusiast mere seconds before the collision, an activity that is prohibited according to Metrolink operating rules. Reporters for Fox News described the accident as the worst of its kind in 15 years. Robert Sanchez, the engineer in question, was killed in the crash.

7. *Facebook updates lead to fatal Chicago pedestrian accident.* 70-year-old Raymond Veloz stepped out of his car to inspect possible damage after a minor fender-bender, only to be hit and killed by a distracted driver who was logged into Facebook at the time of the accident. Details of the 2010 Chicago accident suggest that Araceli Beas was updating her Facebook page via mobile phone at the same time that Veloz placed a call for emergency roadside assistance. Veloz's daughter, Regina Cabrales, argues that Beas was distracted by her use of a mobile device while driving—an illegal act in Illinois since 2009.

6. *One month jail time for texting on the job.* Former San Antonio VIA Metropolitan Transit bus driver Adrian Perez was sentenced to 30 days in jail after evidence was found to confirm that he was using a cell phone to send text messages when he crashed into an SUV back in 2008. The accident injured the driver of the SUV, Betty Jo Hummel, and inspired Perez to speak out against texting and driving as a means of owning up to and repairing his mistakes.

5. *Five months jail time for young texter.* Brittnee Moore, a 20-year-old woman from Waynesburg, PA, was sentenced to jail time after an accident in which Moore's cell phone use caused her to collide with another vehicle in the spring of 2007. The driver of the other vehicle, 16-year-old Hope Maley, was killed in the crash. Moore was found to have been speeding and reaching for her cell phone at the time of the accident. WTAE Pittsburgh reported that Moore would face no less than 5 months in the Greene County Jail for charges of homicide by vehicle, involuntary manslaughter and reckless endangerment.

4. *One year jail time for 20-year-old text & drive motorist.* 20-year-old Heather Marie Anderson was believed to have been using her cell phone to send text messages when she ran a red light and struck another vehicle, killing its driver and incurring a heavy jail sentence back in June of 2010. Anderson's lawyer appealed the sentence, arguing that there was no evidence that his client was in fact texting at the moment of the accident itself. Fredericksburg news outlets reported that in December of 2010, a judge reduced the severity of Anderson's sentence in light of cell phone records regarding her texting activity at the time of the crash. Anderson claims to have put her phone down before the fatal accident occurred, and explained the cause of the crash as "a moment of inattention."

TEENS AND DISTRACTED DRIVING

Have you ever experienced or done any of the following?

	All teens 12–17	Older teens 16–17	Cell users 16–17	Texters 16–17
Been in a car when the driver was texting	48%	64%	70%	73%
Been in a car when the driver used a cell phone in a way that put themselves or others in danger	40%	48%	51%	52%
Talked on a cell phone while driving	n/a	43%	52%	54%
Texted while driving	n/a	26%	32%	34%

Taken from: Mary Madden and Amanda Lenhart, "Teens and Distracted Driving," Pew Research Center, November 16, 2009. www.pewinternet.org.

3. *Six years of prison time for "paying-bills-while-driving" motorist.* California resident Deborah Matis-Engle was driving and paying bills via cell phone when she sped directly into a row of vehicles stopped at a construction site in April of 2007. Engle collided with the car in front of her, causing it to burst into flames and resulting in the death of passenger Petra Winn, 46. *Business Fleet* reported that the judge in the case, based in Redding, CA, sentenced Engle to six years in prison.

2. *Seven-year prison sentence for 22-year-old texting motorist.* In 2004, 22-year-old driver Marcus Johnstone was deleting messages on his cell phone when he hit a power pole. The accident resulted in the death of two teenage girls, and Johnstone was sentenced to six years and nine months in jail as a result of the fatal accident. At the time of his 2006 sentence, Johnstone was the second person in Victoria, Australia, to be charged with culpable and negligent driving as a result of cell phone distraction.

1. *Ten years in prison for texting and driving homicide.* 18-year-old Minnesota resident Kayla Carry was charged with gross negligence and vehicular homicide after a series of 15 text messages sent and received while driving resulted in the wrongful death of 77-year-old Lucille Vogt. According to reports in the Fergus Falls *Daily Journal*, Carry hit Vogt's vehicle in a head-on collision, sustaining serious injuries herself. She will serve up to ten years in prison as a result of the crash. Minnesota is one of the few states to enforce laws prohibiting the sending, receiving or reading of text messages while driving.

> *"It is essential that teenagers understand they face charges associated with sex crimes if they're caught with [sexually explicit] images of underage peers, even if they are underage themselves."*

Teens Can Be Charged with Sex Crimes for Sending Nude Pictures on Cell Phones

Deborah M. Todd

In the following viewpoint, Deborah M. Todd, a reporter for the Pittsburgh Post-Gazette, warns that teens who use their cell phones to send or post sexually explicit pictures of themselves—or of their peers—can be arrested and charged with possessing child pornography, which is a felony, and can be forced to register as sex offenders. The age of the possessor does not make any difference to the law. While in some places it is not enforced against teens, it may be in the future as sending nude pictures becomes increasingly common. Teens need to be aware of the consequences of such actions—not only the immediate legal ones, but the likelihood that the pictures will remain somewhere online and be seen in the future by colleges and prospective employers.

During this season of high school proms and graduations, schools will go as far as bringing the wreckages of fatal highway accidents on campus to stress the dangers of drug and alcohol use to students. However, many of those same schools are ill-equipped when it comes to dealing with the inherent dangers of a ubiquitous and seemingly harmless device—the camera cell phone.

Nationwide, schools and law enforcement agencies are struggling to find ways to deal with teenagers who transmit images of illegal acts, particularly pornographic pictures of themselves or their underage peers, from their cell phones.

On May 20 [2008], 17-year-old Alex Phillips of LaCrosse, Wis., was charged with possessing child pornography, sexual exploitation of a child and defamation after he posted naked pictures of his 16-year-old ex-girlfriend from his cell phone on to MySpace. At Westerville South High School in Westerville, Ohio, at least 30 students received the image of a teenager fondling himself when he sent a cell phone video to female classmates in April.

In Pennsylvania, state police were dispatched to Allentown's Parkland High School in January to remove video and photos of two high school girls from the cell phones of at least 40 students. Closer to home, Thomas Hajzus, principal of Peters Township High School in Washington County, said three female students sent pornographic pictures last school year, and students in Penn Trafford High School said there are multiple porn images of teens circulating in cell phones throughout the district this year. Representatives from the Penn-Trafford School District did not return calls for comment.

State Police Lehigh Trooper Paul Iannace, who assisted at Parkland School District and heads the computer crime investigations division, said pornographic teen images on cell phones is a problem that, as it grows, drains limited resources from other cyber crime investigations.

"There [are] only a handful of [officers] in the state that analyze computer media for evaluation," he explained. "Schools al-

TEENS AND YOUNG ADULTS RESPOND TO SURVEY QUESTIONS ABOUT SEXTING

Which of these have you personally done?

	Teens (13–19)	Young Adults (20–26)	TOTAL
Sent a nude or semi-nude picture/video of yourself to someone	19%	32%	26%
Posted a nude or semi-nude picture/video of yourself online	4%	7%	5%
Received a nude or semi-nude picture/video of himself/herself from someone	31%	46%	39%
Shared a nude or semi-nude picture/video with someone other than the person it was meant for	14%	17%	15%
Had a nude or semi-nude picture/video meant to be private shared with me	29%	32%	30%
None of these	55%	38%	46%

Taken from: *Sex and Tech*, The National Campaign to Prevent Teen and Unplanned Pregnancy, 2008. www.thenationalcampaign.org.

ways ask us if we can [remove pictures] because we're involved day in and day out, but it takes up a lot of our time. We're trying to arrest people for crimes against children."

Trooper Iannace said police in Lehigh County do not normally arrest teens for transmitting images peer-to-peer, but the problem has become so extensive, that may change.

"When you're under 18, you can't have a nude picture. If the image or video depicts someone partially nude who is under 18, it is considered child porn in Pennsylvania. Should we arrest them if they're taking nude pictures and they're sending them to age-appropriate friends? We may have to, because they're using up all of our services."

Against the Law

Law enforcement agents in Allegheny County, however, have never exempted teenagers from arrest for child pornography. In Pittsburgh, a 15-year-old girl was arrested and charged with sexual abuse of children, possession of child pornography and dissemination of child pornography when she posted nude and sexually explicit photos of herself on the Internet in 2004.

Pittsburgh Police Detective Mike Overholt said it is essential that teenagers understand they face charges associated with sex crimes if they're caught with images of underage peers, even if they are underage themselves. Possessing, photographing, selling or transferring sexually explicit images of anyone under 18 is a second-degree felony punishable by up to five years imprisonment in Pennsylvania.

"The law in Pennsylvania is you cannot post sexually explicit pictures of a child. You cannot sell, distribute, display or share them. It's against the law. It doesn't say anything about the age of the person who does it," he said, adding that those convicted could be forced to register as sex offenders.

Detective Overholt agreed with Trooper Iannace that cell phone images are a growing problem, citing a colleague who called it "an epidemic." He said the computer-crimes unit has investigated eight cases this year where porn images had to be erased from teenagers' phones, and he wouldn't be surprised to see more.

"Like one psychologist said, everyone wants to be a star," he said. "We've lost any inhibition that goes with not putting yourself out there."

Jon Nicassio, a 16-year-old freshman at Penn-Trafford High School, agreed that students send naked photos to each other in pursuit of fame. He said he has received explicit images of four female classmates this year, all of whom are under 18. He said the students face little ridicule from classmates and that one student said "she was famous now" after circulating her own photos. His mother, Jennie Nicassio, who blogged about the incident on momssoapbox.com, said she believes "technology has killed society's morals."

Mary Jo Podgurski, director of Washington Hospital Teen Outreach in Washington, Pa., said she believes most young people are pressured by older peers to send sexual images, but knows it's possible some do it to make a name for themselves.

"I hope they're not doing this to be famous, but that's the culture we're living in. The 15 minutes of fame Andy Warhol spoke of is a lot longer now. People go on Jerry Springer and reveal all kinds of personal things. This is not far off from that."

But Dr. Hajzus said blaming the phenomenon on modern culture removes responsibility from families and schools.

"I believe they're excuses for breakdowns in families and schools being able to communicate with kids," he said. "Just because I see a celebrity being nude doesn't mean I'll be nude. My family values will keep me from doing this and the things I learn in school will reinforce those values."

Damage Down the Road

Melissa Orlosky, parent and community program coordinator for the ParentWISE Program of Family Services of Western Pennsylvania, said young people don't consider the social

Underage teens need to be aware that sending nude photos of themselves by cell phone is illegal.
© Steven Puetzer/Photographer's Choice/Getty Images.

consequences such photos could pose in the future, let alone the immediate legal ramifications. Noting that some colleges and businesses now run Google checks on applications, she said educators, law enforcement agents and especially parents must become proactive in teaching child pornography laws to keep kids from making costly mistakes.

"Everyone should be informing kids, parents included. Parents think it's no big deal because it's just a kid thing, but that image is out there forever and keeps re-victimizing this person."

Ms. Podgurski said parents and students should make collaborative efforts to monitor cell phone use.

"Most schools have very strong rules about cell phones, but if you think about it, they're hard to monitor," she said.

She said she has addressed pornographic images in cell phones during her weekly teen peer discussion and has participants sign pledges to "not use cell phones in any way that is disrespectful." But she, too, says stronger efforts need to be made in schools and at home to curb the practice.

"Teens have their own culture, there's no way around it. Part of that culture is cell phones," she said. "The technology is here, we have to work with it."

Beyond the technology, Dr. Hajzus said, parents, schools and community leaders must do more to address self-esteem issues that could lead teenagers to this type of behavior.

"I feel this deals more with a breakdown of self-concept and self-esteem. It leads young girls to seek venues and forums to build their self-concept and esteem because people pay attention to them. Unfortunately, it's the wrong kind of attention," he said.

Technology Gap

Trooper Iannace and Detective Overholt, who both teach about cyber crime in schools and communities, agree that education is key to stemming the problem, but said the fact that the technology is so new makes it difficult to regulate.

"My generation didn't grow up with it, so they have not a clue of the dangers of it or how to tell children to protect themselves. Hopefully the next generation coming up will tell young people of the dangers," said Mr. Iannace.

Detective Overholt said parents should not assume their children are aware of the pitfalls of technology.

"We teach [children] to drive before we give them the car. Do we teach them the do's and don't's of technology before we give them the phone? Did we really teach them how to communicate, or did we just take it for granted that they know?"

11

> *"As it becomes easier to utilize technology, the balance between government interests and individual privacy becomes harder to navigate."*

It Is Legal for Police to Search Cell Phones

Darci G. Van Duzer

In the following viewpoint, Darci G. Van Duzer, a student at the University of Oregon School of Law from 2006 to 2009 and contributing editor of its online law journal, explains that the US Supreme Court and federal circuit courts have suggested that it is not unconstitutional for police to search a cell phone without a warrant, provided it is done during a lawful arrest. Although state laws may differ, the Fourth Amendment's prohibition of unreasonable searches and seizures does not apply to cell phones because during an arrest, it is considered reasonable to search closed containers, and courts have viewed cell phones as similar to closed containers. Also, examining records of the numbers dialed from a particular phone has long been allowed, and text messages are equally subject to quick erasure. However, Van Duzer points out, some legal experts have argued that a person can reasonably expect the content of messages to be private, and so it is uncertain whether cell phones will be classed as mere closed containers by future courts. Research for this viewpoint was conducted by Jay D. Hall, and it was edited by J. Aaron Landau.

Politics just wouldn't be politics without scandals, and the January 2008 scandal in Michigan was a doozy. Detroit Mayor Kwame Kilpatrick, after having testified in open court that he'd never been romantically involved with his chief of staff, found himself in hot water with the law (and, we assume, his wife) when it was revealed that some 14,000 text messages between the two told a very different story. As local prosecutors decided whether to seek perjury charges against the mayor (and as his chief of staff quietly resigned), this executive office romance had many asking some important questions: can the government really search your cell phone? When? Do they need a warrant? And wait, seriously—*fourteen thousand* texts?

It's important to note that Mayor Kilpatrick was caught by virtue of having sent his texts using his government-issued PDA, subject to Michigan's mandatory archiving laws. Your high-school texts are, reassuringly, probably lost to the ether. But what about the messages that are on your phone right now? They may be fair game: recent decisions of the U.S. Supreme Court and several federal circuit courts suggest that cell phone searches, when performed incident to a lawful arrest, *can be* reasonable and constitutional under the Fourth Amendment.

What's a Violation of the Fourth Amendment?

Here's a quick background: the Fourth Amendment to the U.S. Constitution protects individuals against "unreasonable searches and seizures" by government agents and requires "probable cause" before a warrant is issued. In determining what the government can and cannot do, that individual protection has to be balanced with the government's legitimate need to, for example, intrude on an individual's privacy in the name of public safety. The Supreme Court illustrated that balance in *Weeks v. U.S.*

In 1914 a unanimous federal court held that in criminal trials the Fourth Amendment prohibits the use of evidence obtained through warrantless or unreasonable searches. It's known as "the exclusionary rule," and although it seems simple enough, courts have struggled ever since then to define what, exactly, makes such a search "reasonable."

(Note: State laws vary widely, and many states provide more stringent protections than the Fourth Amendment. It's worth keeping in mind that a great deal of search and seizure jurisprudence stems from state law, and is therefore more complex than the analysis provided here. But a general understanding of Fourth Amendment precedent is useful and illustrative of the directions federal and state courts may head.)

What's a Reasonable Search?

Today, the answer to that question hinges on whether or not the search is a violation of an individual's reasonable expectation of privacy. Determining whether the individual's expectation of privacy is "reasonable" involves questions both subjective (does the individual *actually* expect privacy?) and objective (is society ready to recognize that expectation as a reasonable one?). For example, you have the *reasonable* expectation that your personal mail will remain private from the postman's prying eyes, and society generally agrees that no one else should open your mail.

Alternatively, it would be fairly *unreasonable* to expect that anything written on the outside of the envelope you mailed would remain equally private. (This is perhaps why the Mayor and his aide did not exchange their amorous messages via postcards.)

The situation gets a bit more complicated when dealing with a search that occurs during a legitimate arrest. Because law enforcement officers have an interest both in ensuring their own safety (by searching for potential weapons) and in preserving evidence of a possible crime, a search completed "incident to a lawful arrest" is exempted from the warrant requirement and is presumptively "reasonable," thus sidestepping the objective/

Court decisions have suggested it is legal for police to search a suspect's cell phone without a warrant during an arrest. © Chris Hondros/Getty Images News/Getty Images.

subjective test entirely. That leads to the key question: just what *can* an officer search?

Because an officer is presumed to know what is appropriate in the circumstances, whether and how to conduct a search during an arrest is left largely to a police officer's discretion. Of course, not everything an officer finds will be admissible in a criminal proceeding—there are limitations—but during an arrest the officer's discretion is fairly wide, and generally gives an officer power to search your person or the area immediately within your control, regardless of whether you are being arrested for something as minor as offensive littering or as major as multiple homicide. Several courts have held this search can extend to closed containers, glove compartments, packages of cigarettes, and yes, even cell phones.

So, for example, imagine that our heroine Tania Texter gets pulled over for erratic driving. The officer notices that when Tania rolls down the window, the interior of her car reeks of marijuana. During the inevitable arrest, the officer notices a cell phone in

Tania's pocket and decides to scroll through the phone numbers. (He can do that.) The officer is suspicious that Tania has very recently been at a house of a known drug dealer who lives in the neighborhood where the stop was made, so [he scrolls] through her text messages to look for communications. (Yup, he can do that too.) The officer then might have probable cause to believe Tania is involved in narcotics distribution, and search the entire vehicle for contraband.

Can Officials Search a Cell Phone?

The answer, like all great legal answers, is that it depends. Via the "search incident to an arrest" rule, police officers have long had the ability to search "closed containers," any shut box, drawer, or the like. Cell phones, courts have reasoned, are similar enough to closed containers that allowing police to obtain information from them just isn't much of a stretch.

The Fifth Circuit recently held in *U.S. v. Finley* that while an individual may legitimately have a subjective expectation of privacy in his or her cell phone, the "search incident to an arrest" rule provides an officer the authority to search a phone just as he would a closed container on or near the person arrested. By comparing cell phones to closed containers, the court effectively broadened the existing "incident to a lawful arrest" exception to include cell phones, pagers, and PDAs—and potentially other personal technologies as well.

What's the big deal? It has been considered appropriate in certain situations to subpoena information stored on pen registers and phone company records about the phone numbers that people dial. And there does seem to be good reason pagers and cell phones might need to be searched during an arrest: evidence in the form of cell phone numbers dialed can be very quickly, even remotely erased. This doctrine, separate from the "search incident to arrest doctrine," is known as the "probable cause and exigent circumstances doctrine." For example, a California federal court stated:

Because of the finite nature of a pager's electronic memory, incoming pages may destroy currently stored telephone numbers in a pager's memory. The contents of some pagers also can be destroyed merely by turning off the power or touching a button. Thus, it is imperative that law enforcement officers have the authority to immediately search or retrieve, incident to a valid arrest, information from a pager in order to prevent its destruction as evidence. *U.S. v. Chan.*

So what about the text messages? George Washington University Law Professor Orin Kerr tackled this question, arguing that unlike the phone numbers dialed and recorded in [*State v. Smith*, 2009], and unlike the pager-signals used to track the defendant's movement in [*United States v. Knotts*, 1983], text messages represent *content*. This crucial distinction seems to tip the balance in favor of an individual's legitimate expectation of privacy. That theory is buttressed by the Fifth Circuit's opinion in *U.S. v. Finley* that one has a "reasonable expectation of privacy" in one's cell phone text messages as well as numbers; on the other hand, due to the "search incident to arrest" doctrine, the Court still held the search to be lawful—and other federal circuits have yet to address the issue.

Why Does the Extension of This Doctrine Raise So Many Questions?

As it becomes easier to utilize technology, the balance between government interests and individual privacy becomes harder to navigate. The situation may be less dire or alarming than many stories suggest, but the fact remains: as our access to information grows in speed and scope, the avenues a government actor has to reach evidence grows right along with it. Nowhere is that more true than during an arrest: if Fourth Amendment jurisprudence follows the Court of Appeals of the Fifth Circuit in viewing phones and other digital devices as akin to Tupperware stash-boxes, an officer engaged in an otherwise lawful arrest could potentially browse a driver's text messages without fear

Some States Require Police to Obtain a Warrant Before Searching a Cell Phone

The Supreme Court of Ohio ruled [in *State v. Smith*, 2009] that the Fourth Amendment prohibition against unreasonable searches and seizures requires police to obtain a warrant before searching data stored in a cell phone that has been seized from its owner in the course of a lawful arrest. . . . [This ruling applies only in Ohio.]

While acknowledging several federal court decisions during the 1990s that treated electronic pagers and computer memo books as closed containers for search and seizure purposes, Justice [Judith Ann] Lanzinger wrote:

> Each of these cases, however, fails to consider the Supreme Court's definition of 'container' in *Belton*, which implies that the container must actually have a physical object within it. Additionally, the pagers and computer memo books of the early and mid-1990s bear little resemblance to the cell phones of today. Even the more basic models of modern cell phones are capable of storing a wealth of digitized information wholly unlike any physical object found within a closed container. We thus hold that a cell phone is not a closed container for purposes of a Fourth Amendment analysis.

Once the cell phone is in police custody, the state has satisfied its immediate interest in collecting and preserving evidence and can take preventive steps to ensure that the data found on the phone is neither lost nor erased. But because a person has a high expectation of privacy in a cell phone's contents, police must then obtain a warrant before intruding into the phone's contents. . . .

We hold that the warrantless search of data within a cell phone seized incident to a lawful arrest is prohibited by the Fourth Amendment when the search is unnecessary for the safety of law-enforcement officers and there are no exigent circumstances.

Supreme Court of Ohio, Ohio Judicial Center,
www.supremecourt.ohio.gov.

of violating constitutional protections. Although not everyone has 14,000 salacious texts to a chief of staff to worry about, it's a thought-provoking idea nonetheless—and one that brings into clear relief the questions raised as personal digital technology and the Fourth Amendment continue to cross paths.

> *"More than one third of teens with cellphones admit to having stored information on them to look at during a test or texting friends about answers."*

Many Students Use Cell Phones to Cheat on School Tests

Zach Miners

In the following viewpoint, Zach Miners, a reporter for U.S. News & World Report, *reports how common it is for teens to use cell phones to cheat in school. More than a third of those polled admit to having done it, and many don't consider it cheating—they believe texting during exams or using a phone to search the Internet is not the same as looking at someone else's paper. Parents are aware that cheating happens, but only a few of them believe their own teen has cheated. Teachers are developing ways, such as text-matching software, to detect it, but experts say that the best way to discourage cheating is through open discussion of what is expected of students and the presentation of firm guidelines.*

Forget passing handwritten notes underneath desks or inking your arm with essential math formulas before a killer test.

Zach Miners, "One Third of Teens Use Cellphones to Cheat in School," *U.S. News Education Blog*, June 23, 2009. Used by permission.

If students today want to cheat, they have a more insidious tool at their disposal: cellphones. More than one third of teens with cellphones admit to having stored information on them to look at during a test or texting friends about answers, a new survey finds.

And teens' parents, while realistic about the frequency of cheating in schools, might need to overcome their own blind spots: More than 75 percent of parents responding to the survey say that cellphone cheating happens at their children's school, but only 3 percent believe their own teen is using a cellphone to cheat.

"I believe my kids' consciences would prevent them from doing it, as they are good kids deep down," one parent said in an interview for the nationwide online poll, conducted by Common Sense Media, a San Francisco-based education company.

"The results should be a wake-up call for educators and parents," says James Steyer, CEO and founder of Common Sense Media. "These versatile technologies have made cheating easier. The call to action is clear."

That action, Steyer says, should consist of parents and teachers educating themselves on how kids use technology to cheat and then helping students understand that the consequences for online or electronic cheating are just as serious as those for old-fashioned cheating.

But first, adults will have to leap another hurdle. Nearly 1 in 4 students thinks that accessing notes on a cellphone, texting friends with answers, or using a phone to search the Internet for answers during a test isn't cheating.

Some students say that the lack of person-to-person contact in new 21st-century methods of cheating makes it harder for them to feel as if they're doing something wrong. Others see texting during tests simply as helping one another, as opposed to looking at someone else's paper during an exam, which they consider cheating.

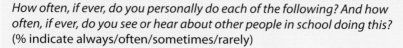

PERCENTAGE OF TEENS WHO USE CELL PHONES TO CHEAT IN SCHOOL

How often, if ever, do you personally do each of the following? And how often, if ever, do you see or hear about other people in school doing this? (% indicate always/often/sometimes/rarely)

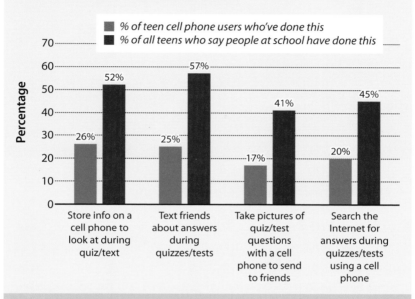

Legend:
- % of teen cell phone users who've done this
- % of all teens who say people at school have done this

Category	% teen users	% all teens
Store info on a cell phone to look at during quiz/text	26%	52%
Text friends about answers during quizzes/tests	25%	57%
Take pictures of quiz/test questions with a cell phone to send to friends	17%	41%
Search the Internet for answers during quizzes/tests using a cell phone	20%	45%

Taken from: "Hi-Tech Cheating: Cell Phones and Cheating in Schools," Common Sense Media, June 18, 2009. www.commonsensemedia.org.

Madeline Jones, a recent graduate of Baylake Pines School in Virginia Beach, Va., says that for papers or online tests, students might use the Web to copy and paste text from other published reports. And for regular in-class exams, she says sneaky students can easily take advantage of the iPhone and its wireless Internet access, as one of her classmates typically did.

Two thirds of responders to the poll—which surveyed 1,013 teens in late May and early June [2009]—say others in their school have cheated with cellphones. More than half admit to using the Internet to cheat.

More than a third of students admit to using cell phones during tests to look up answers.
© Keith Brofsky/UpperCut Images/Getty Images.

Teachers Are Fighting Back

But even as teens advance their electronic cheating strategies, educators are beginning to fight back with their own anticheating technologies, such as text-matching software, biometric equipment, virtual students, and cheatproof tests, experts say.

At the University of Central Florida, for instance, business students now take their tests on cheat-resistant computers in a supersecure testing center. UCF students report much less cheating than students at other campuses.

"We've scared the living daylights out of them," explains Taylor Ellis, associate dean for undergraduate programs and technology at UCF's college of business.

Researchers at Common Sense Media and school administrators say that parents should not assume that kids know what to do or how to behave ethically when it comes to tests on their own. Families should establish open communication about the use of technology in school—including a strict set of guidelines for kids to follow—and understand that kids *are* cheating.

Experts also say that if teachers hold open discussions, issue warnings, and present guidelines for taking tests and writing papers, kids will be more hesitant about cheating.

Jack Lorenz, principal of Ridgewood High School in New Jersey, doesn't think restricting cellphones is the answer.

"I think it's a little bit naive to think that that's going to solve the problem," he said in an interview with CBS News. "If you have a culture in your school where . . . there is an expectation that students are honest about their academic achievements, where students and the administration promote it, I think you decrease the opportunities for students to cheat."

> *"Parents . . . are using a growing number
> of gadgets, software and specially
> equipped cell phones to track kids'
> driving, read their instant messages and
> pinpoint where they're hanging out."*

Parents Are Using Electronic Devices to Keep Track of Teens' Activity

Janine DeFao

In the following viewpoint, Janine DeFao, a staff writer for the San
Francisco Chronicle, *describes some of the ways electronic devices
are being used by parents to track their teenagers. Devices in cars
can reveal driving behavior and speed as well as how far a teen
has driven. GPS (Global Positioning System) devices in cell phones,
and sometimes even in clothing, are being used to keep tabs on
a teenager's location. Some teens do not mind tracking if it is intended to keep them safe, but others believe it is a violation of their
privacy.*

Paige White was surprised when her parents figured out soon
after she started driving last year that she'd gone 9 miles to a
party, not 4 miles to the friend's house she'd told them she was
visiting. It seemed to her almost as if her car was bugged.

Janine DeFao, "Parents Turn to Tech Toys to Track Teens," *San Francisco Chronicle*, July 9,
2006. Used by permission.

It was.

Paige's parents had installed a device in their daughter's SUV that can tell them not only how far she's driven, but how fast and whether she's made any sudden stops or hard turns.

"I was kind of mad because I felt it was an invasion of my privacy," said the Los Gatos resident, now 17.

Parents, some of whom feel outmatched by their offspring in this tech-savvy world, are using a growing number of gadgets, software and specially equipped cell phones to track kids' driving, read their instant messages and pinpoint where they're hanging out.

Move over, Big Brother. Big Mother is in the house.

Simply a New Tool

But cyber-snooping is simply a new tool, experts say. It doesn't resolve the dilemma parents have grappled with for generations: How much free rein do you give children so they can learn the lessons they need to grow up and be independent?

"There's a gap between parents and kids which is unbridgeable: We want them to be safe, and they want to have a good time," said Anthony Wolf, a Massachusetts child psychologist and author of *Get Out of My Life, but First Could You Drive Me and Cheryl to the Mall?: A Parent's Guide to the New Teenager*.

Proponents of the new technology say it can help protect kids—whether from predators lurking online or their own bad driving. But while there may be gains, monitoring also can take a toll.

"The bottom line is, surveillance will cut down somewhat on potential risk behavior kids will engage in, but it is at a cost," Wolf said. "To the extent that you do surveillance, you are potentially interfering with your kids developing responsibility for their own lives."

Bill White had safety in mind when he decided to get the CarChip, made by Davis Instruments in Hayward, for Paige's car when she first got her license.

"I know how I drove when I was in high school," said White, 47.

About the size of a 9-volt battery, the device plugs in beneath a car's dashboard and records driving behavior. The data it collects can be downloaded to a computer, and the device can sound an alarm when the car speeds or accelerates too fast.

While her friends make fun of her for having one, Paige now admits liking the CarChip.

"It helps me watch my speed and keeps me honest," she said.

Tracking Can Save Lives

Supporters say tracking teen driving can save lives. Motor vehicle crashes are the leading cause of death for 15- to 20-year-olds, with 3,620 young drivers killed and 303,000 injured across the country in 2004, according to the National Highway Traffic Safety Administration.

Teen Arrive Alive, a Florida company, offers Global Positioning System-enabled cell phones that allow parents to go online to check the location and speed of a car their child is driving or riding in.

"This is about parents being given tools to better protect their kids. That's not Big Brother. That's parenting," said company spokesman Jack Church, whose 20-year-old son died in a drunken-driving accident in 2000. It took two days to find the car and the young man's body in a ditch.

Church concedes the technology wouldn't have saved his son's life, but said it could have spared him and his wife the agony of searching for two days.

Another company, Alltrack USA, offers a service that e-mails or calls parents if the car they're monitoring exceeds a certain speed or leaves a defined geographic area. DriveCam, which now installs cameras in fleet vehicles, plans to offer a monthly service to parents and teens next year that will let them watch video clips of their driving and receive coaching from driving experts.

Parents have many options for electronically tracking their children's activities. © Erika Kyte/ Photonica/Getty Images.

CarChip-type devices differ from the "black boxes," or event data recorders, installed by manufacturers in many cars to record speed and other data in the seconds before a crash. A California law that limits access to that data does not apply to the types of accessories parents are using.

Privacy Laws Do Not Apply

Nor do privacy laws give kids protection from prying parents.

"In the United States, we sort of think of children as being the property of their parents," said Jennifer Granick, executive director of the Center for Internet and Society at Stanford Law School. "Generally, there's not going to be anything that says parents can't keep tabs on their children."

Another way parents are doing that is with GPS-enabled cell phones. Sprint's Family Locator service allows parents to map the location of their children's cell phones online. Verizon's similar Chaperone service, introduced last month, can send parents text messages if their child leaves a predetermined zone.

SmartWear Technologies in San Diego plans to take GPS monitoring to another level in the fall, offering radio-frequency tags for children's clothing. Already in many items because major retailers use them to track inventory, the tags can be encoded with identification and even a child's medical history. A GPS component will be available next year, said company President Bob Reed.

Orinda mother Melinda Reilly said she is struggling with whether to get her 15-year-old daughter a GPS-enabled cell phone that Reilly can track in the event of the "worst-case scenario" that she couldn't reach the teen by phone.

"When I mentioned it to my daughter, she turned white. She said, 'You wouldn't use it to track me down?' I said, 'That too—but you don't have anything to hide, right?'" said Reilly, 52, who now asks her daughter to check in frequently from her regular cell phone.

"All of these devices, I think, help parents. They're largely not as sophisticated as their kids are in this tech-driven world," added Reilly, who writes a blog urging parents to be more involved in their children's safety. But, she said, "These are very hard choices for parents."

Monitoring Kids Could Backfire

Parent educator and author Jane Bluestein said monitoring kids without cause could backfire, especially when children appear to be following rules and have a good rapport with their parents.

"I think it's going to add a lot of stress to a lot of relationships that really don't need it," said Bluestein, who lives in Albuquerque [New Mexico] and wrote *Parents, Teens and Boundaries: How to Draw the Line.*

"To track kids for the sake of tracking kids—I know it gives parents a sense of control, but I think it points to bigger problems in the relationship: mistrust, a need to control, a need to think for your kids."

It's more important, she said, "for parents to teach kids how to think and act when they're not there." But she said monitoring also could help kids to regain their parents' trust if they've violated it by breaking curfew or lying about where they're going.

Other experts tout the technology as a helping hand for all parents, saying they could be unaware of what their children are up to, especially online.

Internet safety consultant and Bay Area police Officer Steve DeWarns particularly likes software that goes beyond Web filters, which keep children off objectionable sites. Newer software allow parents to track their children's Internet use remotely and can copy instant messages and online chats into e-mails that are sent to parents.

DeWarns knows a father who was tracking his 14-year-old daughter's online correspondence when he learned, while out of town, that a 24-year-old man she'd met online had bought her a bus ticket to visit him out of state. The father thwarted the plan by calling his wife and telling her not to let their daughter out of her sight.

DeWarns even advises parents not to tell older teens they're being monitored, because they may simply avoid the bugged computer.

"The dilemma is, it's like peeking into your kid's diary or journal. The question is: What do you do with that information?" said DeWarns. "It may seem as though parents are going to extremes to monitor their children. However, I'm sure if we asked our parents if they ever listened in on one of our telephone conversations, they would be guilty of it."

Tracking Internet Activity

One Pleasant Hill mother has been using SpectorSoft's eBlaster for about a year to track her sons' online activity, including instant messaging. She's found the boys, 14 and 16, looking at "light porn" and discussing oral sex, and she's ferreted out weekend parties where no adults were going to be home. In those cases, she's made family plans without telling her sons what she knew.

She said the boys think the history function on the computer lets her check up on them. They don't know she has the software or the level of detail she can see, and she asked not to be named for that reason. She said she fears telling them about the software because they may not use the computer as much.

"It has been a chance for my husband and I to bring up subjects that may not come up having to do with sexuality and drugs," she said. "My oldest son said at first he felt we were raiding his privacy. We said the Internet is not a private thing.

"They may fight it, but way deep down, I think they want those boundaries that aren't there for them otherwise on the computer," she said. "It's something they need until they grow up."

Companies that make such software say sales have increased as parents have become more concerned about a range of issues, including pedophiles using the Web to solicit children and teens talking graphically about sex online. SpectorSoft President Doug Fowler said monthly sales of eBlaster have risen from 100 or 200 copies four years ago to 2,500 or 3,000 this year.

No numbers are available for overall use of the various types of monitoring technology, though Church, of Teen Arrive Alive, said sales are lower in more liberal places such as the Bay Area, where parents may be more concerned about their children's privacy.

SpectorSoft recommends that parents tell children they are using the software, Fowler said, but he pointed out parents are not legally required to do so. Other companies are mum on the subject. Fowler said safeguards are built in to keep children from removing the software from the family computer.

Daly City mother Jean Aro said she would have been tempted in the past to know her children's whereabouts at all times, but now that the technology is available, she's not buying.

A Look at Technologies Used to Track Teen Drivers

GPS allows the system to monitor the specific location of the vehicle in real time. GPS data combined with a geospatial database allows the system to monitor roads the vehicle has been driven on or even specific addresses where the vehicle has been parked. . . .

Studies have shown that teens are at much greater risk when one or more peers are present in the vehicle. Thus, it would be helpful to know if a teen is driving with passengers. This is possible with piezoelectric occupant seat sensors that accurately measure passenger weight. . . .

Stereo systems and boisterous behavior should not compete for driver attention. Monitoring in-vehicle sound levels could prove to be an effective way to mitigate distractions from these sources. A microphone can be placed inside the vehicle and connected to a data acquisition board where the audio signals can be processed. If the decibel level reaches an unacceptable limit the system is invoked. Similar technologies are employed in high-end vehicles to ensure the radio is at a constant volume regardless of speed. In newer versions of this technology the driver can be warned, and if the situation persists, parents could be notified or the sound system could be muted. . . .

Cell phone blockers or jammers can disable cell phones so that teens are not able to use the cell phones while driving. Although some technologies that jam cell phone signals are illegal for civilian use, certain technologies that prohibit use of a single phone may be legal. For instance, the Key2SafeDriving device . . . developed by researchers at the University of Utah uses a smart key to transmit a disabling signal to a selected cell phone using Bluetooth or RFID signals, though it does not prohibit 911 calls. The system sends all incoming calls directly to voice mail.

"An Exploration of Vehicle-Based Monitoring of Novice Teen Drivers: Final Report," National Highway Safety Traffic Administration, August 2010, pp. 9–10. www.nhtsa.gov.

"I don't know what kind of message I would be giving my child," said Aro, 51, who has four children and stepchildren ages 13 to 26. "It would have made me mad as hell as a teenager.

"When you know you're being trusted, sometimes you want to show it," she said. "If they feel they're not trusted, they're not going to be trustworthy."

> *"A marginal increase in safety isn't worth forfeiting our civil rights, and adults who balk at being spied on and then turn around and spy themselves are hypocrites."*

Some Teens Consider GPS Tracking a Violation of Their Civil Rights

Steven Barrie-Anthony

In the following viewpoint, Steven Barrie-Anthony, a staff writer for the Los Angeles Times, *discusses arguments against the electronic tracking of teens by their parents. Many teens object to being tracked because it is an unjustified violation of their rights. Some adults agree; one psychiatrist calls it a huge invasion of privacy, and privacy advocates say the desire of parents for so much control is unhealthy. While many parents don't think their children are entitled to privacy, others believe tracking destroys trust within families. But even opponents of electronic tracking say it can be beneficial if families discuss it openly.*

Fifteen-year-old Jordan Murphy loves to play hoops, so after school he and his brother Joshua, 13, jump on bikes and troll their neighborhood in Shawnee, Kan., for pickup games. Often

Steven Barrie-Anthony, "Cellphones: Just a Leash for Children?," *Los Angeles Times*, June 21, 2006. Used by permission.

they pedal through a hectic blind intersection to get to courts at the civic center, and then toss their bags on the ground and start dribbling. They don't hear their cellphone ring-ring-ringing, don't allay the fears of their single mother who's telling herself that all's fine, *probably*, but if only they would just answer the phone. . . .

Then in April, mom Jacqui Fahrnow bought Jordan and Joshua a cellphone from Sprint Nextel that doubles as a tracking beacon. Now if the kids haven't arrived at the civic center or other designated courts by 3:15 in the afternoon, Fahrnow's phone jingles and up pops a color map of their location, replete with street addresses. If they're at or near the courts or at Aunt Valerie's house or the grocery store, Fahrnow doesn't worry; if they're far afield, she knows where to find them. Peace of mind for just $9.99 a month.

"It's like having another set of eyes," says Fahrnow, who owns an office management business. "This will be even more useful when they get older and start driving. With four wheels under you, a lot of things can happen."

Keeping Tabs on the Kids

Sprint Family Locator, which debuted in April [2006], is just one of many newly released cellular services that use global positioning satellites—originally developed for military use—to allow family members to keep tabs on each other via their phones. Disney Mobile, which opened for business earlier this month [June 2006], includes child tracking among its basic features. Verizon Wireless' Chaperone service lets parents enclose up to 10 areas in virtual fencing, and to receive a text message if their children breach a boundary.

This technology isn't cutting-edge, exactly; similar location based services have been marketed with limited success over the last few years, notably Nextel's Mobile Locator designed for companies to track employees. But cellular carriers are in a tizzy to fulfill a Federal Communications Commission mandate that 911

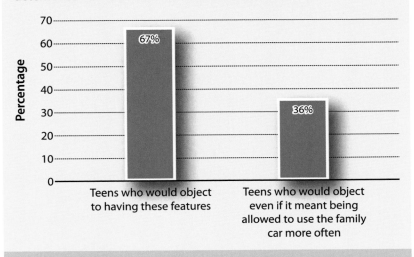

A MAJORITY OF TEENS WILL TOLERATE AUTO DEVICES IF IT MEANS MORE FREEDOM TO DRIVE

Since 2010 new Fords have had a key that prevents the radio from operating unless seat belts are fastened and allows parents to program a maximum audio volume and speed limit. A Harris poll determined how teens would react to these features.

Teens who would object to having these features: 67%

Teens who would object even if it meant being allowed to use the family car more often: 36%

Taken from: "Ford's Innovative Mykey System Helps Teens Drive Safer, Conserve Fuel; Gives Parents Peace of Mind," Ford, January 26, 2011. http://media.ford.com.

operators be able to pin down phone locations—and it stands to reason that they recoup their investment by offering that same capability to subscribers. Carriers make beaucoup bucks, parents like Fahrnow rest easier; everybody wins.

Everybody except the people being tracked, say teens and privacy advocates who peg this trend to an unhealthy desire for control. "What do we get out of this?" says Hunter Ligon, a 16-year-old from Oklahoma City who has discussed the technology with his mom but as of yet remains untracked. "We go to school every day, we work our butts off, and there are such strict limitations on our life already. We need to expand our boundaries, to become more independent, and yet now we have one more thing to pull us down."

Communication technology has become synonymous with youth, says Hunter, who carries a T-Mobile Sidekick II so that he can text and instant message and occasionally even call his friends. Kids these days rarely galavant around the neighborhood until dinnertime, as their parents did; boogeymen on the evening news have driven them indoors, and community has in large part gone virtual. Which makes it particularly galling that technology would become a turncoat, an informer. "Most parents can barely turn on a computer," Hunter says. "They're always asking us for help."

As is the case with Kansas mom Leila Pellant, who couldn't figure out how to set up Sprint Family Locator—and asked her son Spencer, 14, to activate it for her. Spencer obliged, and thenceforth the service "keeps Spencer on point all the time, knowing that I can find out where he is," says Pellant, a real estate agent. "As far as privacy goes, my children don't deserve total privacy."

The argument that it's OK to track kids because it'll keep a few of them from being kidnapped or making mischief is specious reasoning, says 17-year-old Katt Hemman, from Hutchinson, Kan. It's the same argument that the [George W.] Bush administration makes in defending warrantless wiretapping, she says. A marginal increase in safety isn't worth forfeiting our civil rights, and adults who balk at being spied on and then turn around and spy themselves are hypocrites.

Hers is a generation always looking queasily over its shoulder, says Katt, whose parents haven't (yet) signed up for cell tracking but do monitor her Internet activity. "I don't trust as many people as I want to," she says. "I have moments where I don't trust my own family because I feel as if they're reading everything I write on the Internet."

Of course, kids will fight back, much as they do when schools attempt to block access to MySpace and other "noneducational" websites. One teen guesses that encasing his phone in aluminum foil might divert the signal; another especially crafty teen reveals his plan, should mom and dad ever begin phone-surveillance: 1) Tell parents he's going to a friend's house. 2) Go to friend's house. 3) Tie his cellphone to their dog, so it moves around. 4) Leave to live an unobserved existence.

Privacy vs. Safety

But what if your kid is too lazy or obedient to fight back? Or if you track her without her knowledge—and catch her in a lie? How do you explain that you've been watching her through a satellite in the sky? (The Sprint Family Locator notifies kids via a text message when they've been located; other companies, such as Disney Mobile, do not.)

"It's an invasion of privacy in a huge way," says Charles Sophy, a psychiatrist and the medical director for the Los Angeles County Department of Children and Family Services. "You're sending them a message that you don't believe in them, don't trust them to make solid decisions."

Already Sophy has encountered a number of sticky situations surrounding cellphone tracking, "especially with these high-end Hollywood people in L.A.," he says. Tracking without permission often leads to painful family meetings, with everyone—not least of all the parents—apologizing for their misdeeds. Still, Sophy says that in a world of natural and man-made disasters, tracking can "absolutely" be of benefit if prefaced by honest family conversation. Even teens find the safety net appealing if they ignore the Big Brother (or Big Mother) aspect, and some admit that tracking might coax their most out-of-control friends back from the brink.

Of course if kids and the rest of us continue using technology for ever greater self-revelation, the debate over surveillance may be rendered moot. . . . Experts say that mobile social networking, instant messaging and the rest are poised to merge with tracking technology to provide not just virtual access to all friends at all times, but physical access as well. "It will be hard for

science fiction to outpace what's going to happen," says Jonathan Zittrain, professor of Internet governance and regulation at Oxford University. "You'll walk into a cafe in Paris, and ask your cellphone if any of your buddies are in Paris. Or you can ask it if any of the friends of your 10 best buddies are in Paris."

Alan Phillips is an ardent proponent of this revolution. In 2002 he caught his 14-year-old son skateboarding when he was supposed to be at a friend's house, and Phillips promptly founded uLocate Communications, in Massachusetts, to develop location-based services for mobile phones. These days the Phillips family can check each others' locations via a cellphone click (or on the Web) and can even view the rate of speed at which family members are traveling.

"My son plays soccer," Phillips says. "We set up 'geofences' so that when he's coming back from games on the bus, every time his phone comes within five miles of the school, we are alerted. So that we know when to pick him up."

Very convenient; but even Phillips admits that sometimes the ever-present eye is a little much. "I have intentionally turned off my phone to suppress data from my wife," he says. "If I'm leaving late and had told her that I'd meet her somewhere. . . ."

Photo on previous page: Many teens object to being tracked by technology and feel it is a violation of their civil rights. © Sarah L. Voisin/The Washington Post/Getty Images.

> "Harper contended only that she was too
> young and naive to understand that the
> copyrights on published music applied
> to downloaded music."

Teens Can Be Sued for Illegal Sharing of Music Files

The US Court of Appeals' Decision

Edith Brown Clement

In the following court opinion, Edith Brown Clement, a federal judge on the US Court of Appeals for the Fifth Circuit, rules that Whitney Harper must pay the Maverick Recording Company $750 per song for copyright infringement of thirty-seven tracks that she shared illegally on a peer-to-peer network. Harper was very young (between fourteen and sixteen) at the time, and she testified that she had not known then that file sharing was different from listening to music on Internet radio. The lower court, agreeing that this might be true, granted the recording company only $200 per song, but Judge Clement explains that the copyright law specifically states that ignorance makes no difference.

In June 2004, MediaSentry, a company retained by Plaintiffs to investigate the infringement of their copyrights over the

Edith Brown Clement, *Maverick Recording Company v. Harper*, US Court of Appeals 5th Circuit, February 25, 2010.

Internet, identified an individual using a file-sharing program to share 544 digital audio files with other users of a peer-to-peer network. The shared audio files included a number of Plaintiffs' copyrighted sound recordings. By tracing the user's Internet protocol address, Plaintiffs ultimately identified [Whitney] Harper as the individual responsible for the file sharing.

To ensure that each of the 544 audio files was a downloadable file, MediaSentry initiated a download of the entire group. The company captured screen shots showing all of the files that Harper was sharing. It also captured the metadata associated with each file, which included the name of the artist and song. This information allowed Plaintiffs to identify those sound recordings on which they held a copyright. MediaSentry fully downloaded six of the audio files from Harper's "shared folder." Subsequent discovery indicated that Harper had downloaded all of the files from the Internet to the computer without paying for them, and that she had not copied, or "ripped," any of the songs from compact discs that she had bought legally.

During discovery, Plaintiffs examined Harper's computer. The examination showed that its operating system had been reinstalled in 2005. As a result, most of the files present on the computer in 2004, when MediaSentry performed its investigation, had been overwritten. The forensic examination did show that three file-sharing programs had been installed and used on the computer, including a program known as LimeWire, which had been used after the operating system was reinstalled. It also revealed a new cache of approximately 700 recordings downloaded since the reinstallation. Fifteen of the copyrights that Plaintiffs' second amended complaint alleged that Harper infringed came from this newly discovered cache. . . .

The district court denied Plaintiffs' request for statutory damages. Plaintiffs had requested the minimum damages of $750 per infringed work set forth in [the Copyright Act]. Harper asserted that her infringement was "innocent" under [the law], which provides that "where the infringer sustains the burden of

Illegal music sharing on peer-to-peer networks can be the basis for a copyright infringement lawsuit. © Laurence Dutton/Photographer's Choice/Getty Images.

proving . . . that [she] was not aware and had no reason to believe that . . . her acts constituted an infringement of copyright, the court in its discretion may reduce the award of statutory damages to a sum of not less than $200." Harper averred that she thought her actions were equivalent to listening to an Internet radio station. The district court found that whether her infringe-ment was "innocent" presented a disputed issue of material fact.

The district court denied each party's motion for reconsid-eration. In doing so, it clarified its finding that Harper infringed Plaintiffs' exclusive rights to both reproduce and distribute the 37 songs on which they held a copyright.

Reserving the right to appeal the district court's legal con-clusion on the innocent infringer issue if Harper appealed, Plaintiffs moved for entry of judgment in the amount of $200 for each infringed work—the minimum amount due from an in-nocent infringer. The court granted Plaintiffs' motion and en-tered judgment against Harper. Harper appealed, and Plaintiffs cross-appealed. . . .

Sufficiency of the Evidence

Harper argues that Plaintiffs did not present sufficient evidence for the district court to find that 31 of the 37 audio files at issue existed on her computer. She does not contest the existence of the six audio files that MediaSentry downloaded in full over the peer-to-peer file-sharing network in 2004. She also cannot contest the existence of the 15 audio files that were part of the cache of ap-proximately 700 songs discovered on Harper's hard drive in 2008. The issue, then, is whether Plaintiffs made an undisputed show-ing that Harper had downloaded the remaining 16 audio files.

Harper's argument relies on the computer forensic expert's inability to recover complete copies of the 16 contested audio files when the expert searched her computer's hard drive in 2008. That inability was due to the 2005 reinstallation of the comput-er's operating system, which overwrote most of the audio files present in 2004. Harper asserts that the 2008 forensic evidence is inconclusive and that a jury could find that the file remnants discovered in the 2008 examination were something other than downloaded audio files.

Harper's argument ignores the voluminous and undisputed evidence that she downloaded and shared the 16 contested audio files. MediaSentry's screen shots of Harper's "shared folder" indicate that she was sharing the contested audio files from her computer in 2004. MediaSentry also initiated downloads of the audio files to verify their existence and recovered metadata from which it could identify the artist and song title of each file.

Harper submitted no evidence that calls into question Plaintiffs' showing that she had downloaded the audio files. In her deposition, she did not deny that she had downloaded them. She also testified that she had not copied any of the recordings to her computer from compact discs that she purchased, and she acknowledged using a peer-to-peer file-sharing network and stated that she recognized "some of the songs . . . as music I listened to and may have downloaded to the computer."

The uncontroverted evidence is more than sufficient to compel a finding that Harper had downloaded the files: there was no evidence from which a factfinder could draw a reasonable inference that Harper had not downloaded them or that they were something other than audio files. . . .

Copyright Infringement

Section 106 of the Copyright Act grants copyright owners the exclusive right "to do and to authorize," inter alia [among other things], the reproduction of "the copyrighted work in copies or phonorecords," the preparation of "derivative works based upon the copyrighted work," and the distribution of "copies or phonorecords of the copyrighted work to the public by sale or other transfer of ownership, or by rental, lease, or lending." . . . Plaintiffs alleged that Harper had violated their copyrights in two ways: first, by reproducing the copyrighted audio files, and second, by making them available to others, which Plaintiffs argue is tantamount to "distribution." The district court found that the undisputed evidence showed Harper had done both.

Harper argues that making audio files available to others by placing them in a "shared folder" accessible by users of a peer-to-peer file-sharing network does not constitute "distribut[ion]." We need not address the "making available" argument at this time, however, because Harper did not appeal the district court's finding that she had infringed Plaintiffs' copyrights by downloading, and hence reproducing, the audio files. Because Plaintiffs only seek minimum statutory damages, the question before the court is whether Harper's actions violated the Copyright Act, not how or to what extent they violated it. . . .

Due Process

Harper contends that the statutory scheme of damages for copyright violations outlined in [the law], as applied to her, violates due process by imposing grossly excessive damages. She argues that, at the time of the infringement, she was young and did not know that what she was doing was unlawful, and that fining her several hundred dollars per song for illegal downloading does not comport with substantive due process.

Harper, however, waived her constitutional challenge by failing to raise it below in a manner that would allow the district court to rule on it. . . .

In her opposition to Plaintiffs' motion for summary judgment, Harper stated that she had notified the district court of her intent to challenge the constitutionality of the Copyright Act. She then presented the whole of her constitutional argument: "Whitney Harper believes that the copyright law, as being applied by the plaintiff, is unfair and over-reaching and exacts an unreasonable punishment." Harper did not cite any provision of the Constitution or explain why the punishment was so unreasonable that it violated due process. . . .

"Innocent Infringer" Defense

In denying Plaintiffs' motion for summary judgment as to damages, the district court held that there was a genuine issue of material fact as to whether Harper was an innocent infringer. The innocent infringer defense gives the district court discretion to reduce the minimum statutory damages from $750 to $200 per infringed work if it finds that the infringer "was not aware and had no reason to believe that his or her acts constituted an infringement of copyright." Harper averred in an affidavit that she did not understand the nature of file-sharing programs and that she believed that listening to music from file-sharing networks was akin to listening to a non-infringing Internet radio station. The district court ruled that this assertion created a triable issue as to whether Harper's infringement was "innocent" under [the Copyright Act].

Assuming arguendo [for the sake of argument] that Harper made a prima facie case [with sufficient evidence to support the legal claim] that she was an innocent infringer, we hold that the defense was unavailable to her as a matter of law. The innocent infringer defense is limited . . . with one exception not relevant here, when a proper copyright notice "appears on the published . . . phonorecords to which a defendant . . . had access, then no weight shall be given to such a defendant's interposition of a defense based on innocent infringement in mitigation of actual or statutory damages."

The district court acknowledged that Plaintiffs provided proper notice on each of the published phonorecords from which the audio files were taken. It found, however, that regardless of Harper's access to the published phonorecords, such access would not necessarily put her on notice of the copyrights: "a question remains as to whether Defendant knew the warnings on compact discs were applicable in this [file-sharing network] setting." The court discounted the argument "that one need only have access to some CD and see that the recording is subject to copyright" to bar the innocent infringer defense, because knowledge that some CDs are copyrighted does "little to establish that, as a matter of law . . . an individual knew that she was accessing copyright material from an entity that did not have permission to distribute such material." In her brief opposing summary judgment and brief on appeal, and at oral argument, rather than contest the fact of "access," Harper con-

PERCENTAGE OF TEENS WHO DOWNLOAD MUSIC WITHOUT PAYING FOR IT

A 2011 survey conducted by Piper Jaffray indicates that a substantial percentage of teens download music without paying for it. Of those surveyed, a greater percentage would rather pay a monthly subscription fee than a per-song fee.

	Fall 2007	Spring 2008	Fall 2008	Spring 2009	Fall 2009	Spring 2010	Fall 2010	Spring 2011
Teens who download music	82%	85%	80%	82%	83%	82%	76%	77%
Download using P2P (free) file sharing	64%	61%	60%	60%	57%	57%	66%	65%
Purchase tracks online	36%	39%	40%	40%	43%	43%	34%	35%
Consider paying $.99 per track	21%	27%	18%	25%	20%	11%	21%	22%
Consider paying $15/mo for subscription	36%	38%	37%	46%	38%	34%	35%	37%

Taken from: "Only 22% of High Schoolers Want to Pay 99¢ A Song," Hypebot.com, April 2011.

tended only that she was too young and naive to understand that the copyrights on published music applied to downloaded music.

These arguments are insufficient to defeat the interposition of the limitation on the innocent infringer defense. Harper's reliance on her own understanding of copyright law—or lack thereof—is irrelevant. . . . The plain language of the statute shows that the

Remarks by the US Secretary of Commerce on Music Piracy

As Vice President [Joe] Biden has said on more than one occasion, "Piracy is flat, unadulterated theft," and it should be dealt with accordingly.

This isn't just an issue of right and wrong. This is a fundamental issue of America's economic competitiveness.

As the president [Barack Obama] has said before, America's "single greatest asset is the innovation and ingenuity and creativity of the American people. It is central to our prosperity and it will only become more so in this century."

Our founding fathers understood this as well as anyone, which is why they put in place a set of rules and laws to reward and protect the ideas and inventions of the artists, engineers and scientists who create them.

But this copyright and patent framework needs to evolve to meet the evolving challenges of the 21st century.

Recently, I've had a chance to read letters from award winning writers and artists whose livelihoods have been destroyed by music piracy. One letter that stuck out for me was a guy who said the songwriting royalties he had depended on to "be a golden parachute to fund his retirement had turned out to be a lead balloon."

This just isn't right.

And this administration is doing everything it can to ensure our creators and our innovators are compensated for the great work that they do.

*Gary Locke, Remarks at Intellectual Property
Enforcement, Belmont University, Nashville,
Tennessee, US Department of Commerce,
August 30, 2010. www.commerce.gov.*

infringer's knowledge or intent does not affect its application. Lack of legal sophistication cannot overcome a properly asserted limitation to the innocent infringer defense. . . .

In short, the district court found a genuine issue of fact as to whether Harper intended to infringe Plaintiffs' copyrights, but that issue was not material: [the statute] forecloses, as a matter of law, Harper's innocent infringer defense. Because the defense does not apply, Plaintiffs are entitled to statutory damages. And because Plaintiffs requested the minimum statutory damages under [the law], Harper's culpability is not an issue and there are no issues left for trial. Plaintiffs must be awarded statutory damages of $750 per infringed work.

> *"Until something is figured out so that authors can still get paid so they can make a living, readers just taking what they want will result in a lot of authors just not being able to write anymore."*

An Author Discusses the Harm Caused by E-book Piracy

Personal Narrative

Kimberly Pauley

In the following personal narrative, Kimberly Pauley, the author of two popular young adult novels, describes why she believes the illegal downloading of her novels' e-book editions is hurting her. More people have obtained illegal copies of her second book than have bought it, she says, which may be the reason why it has not sold as well as her first one. The problem goes beyond the income lost on those books; if the book does not sell well enough, her publisher may not accept more manuscripts from her. She expresses the hope that when people are thinking about downloading content illegally, they will remember the consequences for the person who produced that work and refrain from such actions.

Kimberly Pauley, "So, What Do I Think About Book Piracy, Anyway?," KimberlyPauley .com, January 12, 2011. Used by permission of the author.

Today on Twitter, the fab Sarah Rees Brenna (*Demon's Lexicon*) awoke to a "fan" tweeting her that she had illegally downloaded a copy of her book because it wasn't available in ebook form in her country. It is, however, actually available in print. The fan furthermore goes on to explain that she never illegally downloads anything and, *of course*, plans on buying the book if it actually becomes available. Then she seemed genuinely surprised that Sarah was (understandably) rather put out that someone had just told her to her face that she'd stolen a copy of her book.

I don't know. Maybe she will actually go out and buy a copy some day. It's hard to say. But probably 99% of people who illegally download books *don't* go out and buy a copy. And they are killing books every day. . . .

My first book (*Sucks to Be Me*) was pretty well received and did earn out the advance. It was a YALSA [Young Adult Library Services Association] Quick Pick and is still being sold in stores (now in paperback) over two years later. It didn't hit a bestseller list or anything, but it's done well for a first book. It did well enough that my publisher wanted to buy a second book in the series (*Still Sucks to Be Me*), which came out in May 2010.

Herein lies the rub. The first book didn't come out in ebook form until after it had already been out for a good long time (for whatever reasons; I'm not really sure why). There were some illegal downloads (where someone had literally translated a copy by hand into another language, it looked like), but nothing too serious. However, the second book released in hardcover *and* ebook form pretty much at the same time.

There have been thousands and thousands of illegal downloads of the second book. THOUSANDS. The actual real sales have been okay, but not as good as the first book (though the general reception as far as reviews, emails from fans, etc. has been about the same). At least once a week I get a new Google alert about a new download site with illegal copies of the book for download. All I can do is forward them on to the legal department of my publisher (and I'll be honest, I don't always forward them on even though I should . . . it's just depressing since it feels like no matter what you do, it doesn't make a difference). But as soon as one link is killed, three more pop up. Just *one* download site had over 22,000 illegal downloads of the book and it looked like it had just been up for a week. Just. One. Week.

Essentially, more people have illegally downloaded the second book than have purchased it (as of my first royalty statement).

Book Sales Affect Chance of Future Publication

Guess what, peeps. That's a problem. It's not so much the money, though I admit that hurts as well (I am NOT rich and paying for a part time nanny for The Max is an essential but sometimes hard to justify reality for me as a writer—I challenge you to write anything readable while entertaining a two year old). It's the fact that I very well may not get to write a third book in the series because actual sales aren't blowing my publisher away. Obviously people are reading the book and *want* to read it. I get emails pretty much every day with people asking when a third *Sucks to Be Me* book will be coming out (and thank you, to all of you who ask). My answer right now is just that I hope one will. I haven't written it even though I've got a plot because it's not worth my time to write it unless I can get it published. I've got other books to work on. And my publisher isn't going to publish it unless sales are better, no matter how much my editor would love to do so. . . .

And, of course, there's always the worry that this may affect future books of mine. Right now, the first book is still selling and I keep seeing new reviews of it. Which is great. I have no idea how the second one will wind up, not with all the illegal downloads that go on every day. For some reason, I don't get nearly as many illegal download alerts on the first book, which I am thankful for.

The whole thing scares me. I love writing. But I can't afford to do it unless people actually buy the books. Will prospective publishers look at my second book sales and go "Meh"? I don't know. I certainly hope not. But they don't see those readers that obtained the book through an illegal download . . . and even if they did, why would they care? Those aren't people buying the book.

When I've posted about this before, one fellow (besides telling me I should be "happy" about it (!!)) kept harping about how the market is changing. Yes, I completely understand that. But until something is figured out so that authors can still get paid so they can make a living, readers just taking what they want will result in a lot of authors just not being able to write anymore. And that sucks for everyone. And I'm not talking just me. I'm talking about authors in general. . . . Book piracy is hurting lots of authors all over the world, every day. . . .

Book Piracy Hurts Authors

I've been doing a lot of thinking about this and also reading up on it from all perspectives. . . .

First off, I suppose you should understand where I'm coming from. I think I can safely label myself as a mid-list author right now. That means that my books (all two of them so far . . .) are doing well, but aren't bestsellers. The average person on the street has no idea who I am. My author-ly career is really just starting out. I am not well-established. Just because I write a book doesn't mean it will get sold to a publisher (I wish!). I do have a fan base (some of whom write me regularly and boy, do I love those guys), but if I have a book signing, I have no worries about being mobbed. I have no guarantees and should probably tread carefully (which really means I probably shouldn't even blog about stuff like this since we authors are *supposed* to be all Stepford Wife-y and present a smiley, happy, always positive-everything-is-A-Okay face to the world. But I already opened my big mouth, so I might as well soldier on). I am a professional when it comes to my writing and I do take it seriously, but I'm also a mom to a toddler, so that changes my priorities some.

My goal is to be able to keep writing, primarily YA [young adult] books, but also perhaps some adult or middle grade novels. I'd like to get to the point where I can turn out two books a year, maybe three (given how I work, I don't think I could do more than three in a year, not without seriously impinging on my family life and/or the quality of the books I write). I am not the world's best writer and I'm not the worst either. I'm pretty good, but I'm still learning every day.

So that, in a rather largish nutshell, is me.

Do I think book piracy is hurting me?

Yes, I do.

Do I know positively, absolutely that book piracy is hurting me?

No, I don't.

I don't know that it *isn't* either. I have, really, no way of knowing. No one does. It's the nature of the beast. Take those 24,503 people who downloaded a copy of the second book from that one website that week. How many of them would have bought the book if an illegal download wasn't available? How many would have borrowed it from a library? How many would have just forgotten about it completely? How many would have never even heard of me? Heck, how many thought they were downloading a copy of that Avenue Q song instead and wound up with a surprise? I have no idea.

So, while I *think* book piracy is hurting me (and other authors, some of whom have more concrete numbers than I do), I have no idea *how much* it is hurting me.

Do I think book piracy is wrong?

Yes. Stealing is wrong. Though I also don't think it is a completely black and white issue. I mean, hey, almost no issue is. I think that people in the U.S. who have all the access in the world to U.S. published books (in many formats) have really no excuse. Get thee to a library if you don't want to buy a book. Borrow it from a friend.

People outside the U.S., depending on which country they are in, can face many obstacles, not the least of which is just plain accessibility. Do I think it's okay for someone, say, in New Zealand to download an illegal copy of my book because it's hard for them to get it or because it's really expensive? No, not really. Because illegally downloading a copy is a quick fix (for that person) but does nothing to solve the larger issues of availability and cost. Complain to publishers. Make your voices heard. Illegally downloading a copy doesn't tell anyone anything and won't change anything . . . other than possibly helping put a nail in the coffin of an author's career. But do I understand the temptation to do so? Yes, of course I do. . . .

Do I think illegal downloads have had an impact on the sales of my second book (and on the status of a third Sucks to Be Me *book)?*

Yes, I do think so. Of course, it's not the only thing that's had an impact. Like I mentioned above, sales of the second book have been okay, they just haven't been "knock your socks off." I mean, I did earn out my advance. I think book piracy has been part of the issue, but also the general economic problems in the U.S. (and elsewhere) have contributed. And it *is* a vampire book and that market seems to be cooling now that *Twilight* fever has dropped down (boy, seriously, if I could go back in time to when I was writing my first book back before *Twilight* came out, I probably would have told myself to work on anything *but* a vampire novel . . . really it has probably been both a curse and a blessing). The book has been well received as far as reviews go (about the same as the first book) and the fan mail levels have been pretty similar too.

So, while I do believe that book piracy has had a detrimental impact on the second book, I cannot tell you *how much* of an impact it has had. . . .

What about the whole book piracy thing?

What about it? Honestly, there's not much of anything I *can* do about it. I probably shouldn't have bothered posting about it, but I'm human and I was feeling rather raw and sad on the whole thing and I also wanted to support my author-y friends. . . . I do hope that perhaps some people will have read through some of these posts and the next time they're thinking about illegally downloading something . . . they don't. I think that's about all I can hope for.

So, that's it?

Yup. As they say, that's that. I am going to try very, very, very hard not to say anything else about this subject (seriously, if I even look like I'm going to blog about it again, just hit me upside the head with a slab of bacon or whatever is handy). I do not have any answers. And I am not the Great and Powerful Oz. I don't have any solutions to suggest, especially not any that would cover all the myriad versions of this particularly thorny issue in all regions. It's a multi-headed beast, this thing.

I just hope I can keep on writing. I'll do my best to make sure that I can.

Organizations to Contact

The editors have compiled the following list of organizations concerned with the issues debated in this book. The descriptions are derived from materials provided by the organizations.

Common Sense Media
650 Townsend, Suite 435
San Francisco, CA 94103
(415) 863-0600 • fax: (415) 863-0601
website: www.commonsensemedia.org

Common Sense Media is a national, nonpartisan organization dedicated to improving the lives of kids and families by providing information and education about media and technology. Its website provides reviews of movies, games, and apps, plus advice on issues such as digital citizenship, family media management, digital harassment, and cyberbullying. Materials for parents and schools are also available.

Connect Safely
e-mail: admin@connectsafely.org
website: www.connectsafely.org

Connect Safely is a project of Tech Parenting Group, a nonprofit organization based in Palo Alto, California, and Salt Lake City, Utah. It is an interactive resource for parents, teens, and educators engaged and interested in youth safety on the web. Its website contains more about mobile devices than most sites that deal with Internet safety, including cell phones, GPS location-sharing, video gaming, and sexting.

CTIA—The Wireless Association
1400 16th Street, NW, Suite 600, Washington, DC 20036

(202) 736-3200 • fax: (202) 785-0721
website: www.ctia.org

CTIA—The Wireless Association is an international nonprofit organization that represents the wireless communications industry and advocates on behalf of its members at all levels of government. CTIA also coordinates the industry's voluntary efforts to provide consumers with a variety of choices and information regarding their wireless products and services. Its website includes a position paper on "Protecting Children in Mobile Environments," safety tips, and a video about the dangers of distracted driving.

Cyberbullying Research Center

School of Criminology and Criminal Justice
Florida Atlantic University
5353 Parkside Drive
Jupiter, FL 33458-2906
e-mail: hinduja@cyberbullying.us
website: www.cyberbullying.us

The Cyberbullying Research Center provides up-to-date information about the nature, extent, causes, and consequences of cyberbullying among adolescents, defined as willful infliction of harm through the use of computers, cell phones, and other electronic devices. Its website serves as a clearinghouse of information concerning the ways adolescents use and misuse technology, and includes information about cell phone safety.

Entertainment Merchants Association (EMA)

16530 Ventura Boulevard, Suite 400
Encino, CA 91436-4551
(818) 385-1500 • fax: (818) 385-0567
website: www.entmerch.org

The EMA is a nonprofit international trade association dedicated to advancing the interests of the companies that sell and/or rent DVDs, computer and console video games, and digitally distributed versions of these products. The EMA was the plaintiff in the 2011 Supreme Court case in which laws restricting the sale of violent video games were ruled unconstitutional. Its website contains facts about the video game industry and its ratings program, plus a position statement on piracy.

National Safety Council (NSC)

1121 Spring Lake Drive
Itasca, IL 60143-3201
(800) 621-7615 • fax: (630) 285-1315
website: www.nsc.org

The National Safety Council seeks to save lives by preventing injuries and deaths at work, in homes and communities, and on the roads through leadership, research, education, and advocacy. Its website has a section on road safety with information about teen driving and distracted driving, including a downloadable report, *Understanding the Distracted Brain,* that explains why multitasking interferes with driver performance.

National Youth Rights Association (NYRA)

1101 15th Street NW, Suite 200
Washington, DC 20005
(202) 835-1739
website: www.youthrights.org

NYRA is a youth-led national nonprofit organization dedicated to fighting for the civil rights and liberties of young people. NYRA has more than seven thousand members representing all fifty states. It seeks to lower the voting age, lower the drinking age, repeal curfew laws, and protect student rights.

Recording Industry Association of America (RIAA)

1025 F Street NW, 10th Floor
Washington, DC 20004
(202) 775-0101
website: www.riaa.org

The RIAA is a trade group that represents the US recording industry. Its mission is to foster a business and legal climate that supports and promotes members' creative and financial vitality. Its website contains a downloadable guide titled "Young People, Music and the Internet," as well as news about its efforts to combat piracy, information for parents, and a list of legal music sites. There is also an FAQ section for students doing reports.

Remember Alex Brown Foundation

PO Box 55
Wellman, TX 79378
(806) 893-2625
website: www.rememberalexbrownfoundation.org

The Remember Alex Brown Foundation was established by the television show *Extreme Makeover Home Edition* and Palm Harbor Homes to publicize the dangers of texting while driving. The foundation also raises funds to support presentations to schools by the parents of teenager Alex Brown, who was killed in a car accident as a result of texting while driving. Its website contains information about Alex, a video by her parents, and a form to be signed by teens who pledge not to text and drive.

Student Press Law Center (SPLC)

1101 Wilson Boulevard, Suite 1100
Arlington, VA 22209-2275
(703) 807-1904
website: www.splc.org

The SPLC is a legal assistance agency devoted to educating high school and college journalists about the rights and responsibilities embodied in the First Amendment and supporting the student news media in their struggle to cover important issues free from censorship. Its website also contains information about legal issues associated with the use of cell phones.

For Further Reading

Books

Naomi Baron, *Always On: Language in an Online and Mobile World*. New York: Oxford University Press, 2010.

Mark Bauerlein, *The Dumbest Generation: How the Digital Age Stupefies Young Americans and Jeopardizes Our Future*. New York: Tarcher, 2008.

Susan Brooks-Young, *Teaching With the Tools Kids Really Use: Learning With Web and Mobile Technologies*. Thousand Oaks, CA: Corwin Press, 2010.

Vickie Courtney, *Logged On and Tuned Out: A Non-Techie's Guide to Parenting a Tech-Savvy Generation*. Nashville, TN: B&H Books, 2007.

Anastasia Goodstein, *Totally Wired: What Teens and Tweens Are Really Doing Online*. New York: St. Martin's, 2007.

Thomas A. Jacobs, *Teen Cyberbullying Investigated: Where Do Your Rights End and Consequences Begin?* Minneapolis, MN: Free Spirit Publishing, 2010.

Liz Kolb, *Cell Phones in the Classroom: A Practical Guide for Educators*. Eugene, OR: International Society for Technology in Education, 2011.

Robin M. Kowalski, Susan P. Limber, and Patricia W. Agatston, *Cyber Bullying: Bullying in the Digital Age*. Maiden, MA: Blackwell, 2008.

Susan Maushart, *The Winter of Our Disconnect: How Three Totally Wired Teenagers (and a Mother Who Slept with Her iPhone) Pulled the Plug on Their Technology and Lived to Tell the Tale*. New York: Tarcher, 2011.

Lisa Nielsen and Willyn Webb, *Teaching Generation Text: Using Cell Phones to Enhance Learning.* San Francisco, CA: Jossey-Bass, 2011.

Michael Osit, *Generation Text: Raising Well-Adjusted Kids in an Age of Instant Everything.* New York: AMACOM, 2008.

Kevin Roberts, *Cyber Junkie: Escape the Gaming and Internet Trap.* Center City, MN: Hazelden Publishing, 2010.

Larry D. Rosen, *Rewired: Understanding the iGeneration and the Way They Learn.* New York: Macmillan, 2010.

Gwenn Schurgin O'Keeffe, *CyberSafe: Protecting and Empowering Kids in the Digital World of Texting, Gaming, and Social Media.* Elk Grove Village, IL: American Academy of Pediatrics, 2010.

Don Tapscott, *Grown Up Digital: How the Net Generation Is Changing Your World.* New York: McGraw-Hill, 2009.

Annie Winston, *A Father's Sexting Teen: The Brian Hunt Story.* Irvine, CA: Tri-Net Publishing, 2010.

Periodicals and Internet Sources

Lauren Barack, "The Kindles Are Coming: Ereaders and Tablets Are Springing Up in Schools—and Librarians Are Leading the Way," *School Library Journal,* March 1, 2011. www.libraryjournal.com.

Mark Bauerlein, "Another Problem with Texting," *Chronicle of Higher Education,* June 24, 2009. http://chronicle.com.

Ken Belson, "Keeping Tabs on Your Teen," *New York Times,* September 30, 2007.

Julie Bosman, "E-Readers Catch Younger Eyes and Go in Backpacks," *New York Times,* February 4, 2011.

Andy Carvin, "Should Principals Be Allowed to Review Students' Cell Phone Records?" PBS Teachers, July 7, 2006. www.pbs.org.

Larry Copeland, "Teens Missing Message on Road Texting Risk," *USA Today*, September 20, 2010.

Peter Daut, "Teen Wants $7.5 Million from School District for Cell Phone Search," MyFOXdfw, August 2, 2010. www.myfoxdfw.com.

Rick Docksai, "Teens and Cell Phones: Cell Phones Can Be Noisy and Distracting. But They Can Also Be an Aid to Learning," *The Futurist*, January 1, 2009.

An Exploration of Vehicle-Based Monitoring of Novice Teen Drivers: Final Report, National Highway Safety Traffic Administration, August 2010. www.nhtsa.gov.

A Generation Unplugged, Harris Interactive, September 12, 2008. http://files.ctia.org.

Adam M. Gershowitz, "The iPhone Meets the Fourth Amendment," University of Houston Law Center, January 15, 2008. http://papers.ssrn.com.

How Teens Use Media, The Nielsen Company, June 2009. http://blog.nielsen.com.

Adrian Kingsley-Hughes, "Copyright Laws and Piracy—Where Do You Stand?" ZDNet, April 10, 2007. www.zdnet.com.

Amanda Lenhart et al., *Teens, Video Games and Civics*, Pew Research Center, September 16, 2008. www.pewinternet.org.

Frank LoMonte, "AG Cuccinelli's Go-Ahead to Search Student Cell-Phones Raises Fourth Amendment Questions," Student Press Law Center, November 29, 2010. www.splc.org.

Mary Madden and Amanda Lenhart, "Teens and Distracted Driving," Pew Research Center, November 16, 2009. www.pewinternet.org.

Corbin Newlyn, "GPS Tracking Devices—Teens vs Parents, Law Enforcement vs Invasion of Privacy," Tech-Seeker, March 14, 2011. http://tech-seeker.com.

Stefanie Olsen, "Technology & the Law: How Does the Constitution—Written 200 Years Before Facebook and Texting—Apply to the Digital World?," *New York Times Upfront*, September 6, 2010.

Matt Richtel, "Driven to Distraction: As Multitasking Behind the Wheel Takes a Growing Toll, Lawmakers Are Cracking Down on Texting While Driving," *New York Times Upfront*, January 18, 2010.

Victoria J. Rideout, Ulla G. Foehr, and Donald F. Roberts, *Generation M2: Media in the Lives of 8- to 18-Year-Olds*, Kaiser Family Foundation, January 2010. www.kff.org.

Sex and Tech: Results from a Survey of Teens and Young Adults, National Campaign to Prevent Teen and Unplanned Pregnancy, 2008. www.thenationalcampaign.org.

Supreme Court of Ohio Visitor Education Center, "Cell Phones: Search and Seizure, Analyzing a Case," 2010. www.sconet .state.oh.us.

John D. Sutter, "Report: iPhones Secretly Track Their Users' Locations," CNN.com, April 21, 2011. www.cnn.com.

Zoe Tillman, "Wise High Student: Security Guard 'Hit Me' Over Cell Phone; Family Is Considering Legal Action," Gazette.net, December 2, 2010. www.gazette.net.

Barbara Valentine and Steven Bernhisel, "Teens and Their Technologies in High School and College: Implications for Teaching and Learning," *Journal of Academic Librarianship*, November 2008. www.linfield.edu.

Kim Zetter, "School RFID Plan Gets an F," Wired.com. February 10, 2005. www.wired.com.

Index